190

4

# YOU CAN
# MAKE IT HAPPEN

>>>>>>>>>>>>>

*A Nine-Step Plan for Success*

**Stedman Graham**

SIMON & SCHUSTER

SIMON & SCHUSTER
Rockefeller Center
1230 Avenue of the Americas
New York, NY 10020

SIMON & SCHUSTER and colophon are registered trademarks
of Simon & Schuster Inc.

Designed by Irving Perkins Associates

Manufactured in the United States of America

10   9   8   7   6   5   4   3   2   1

Library of Congress Cataloging-in-Publication Data

Graham, Stedman.
    You can make it happen: a nine-step plan for success/Stedman Graham.
      p.   cm.
    1. Success in business.   2. Success.   3. Minorities.   I. Title.
    HF5386.G655   1997
    650.1—dc21                                                        96-45457
                                                                          CIP

ISBN 0-684-81448-X

# Acknowledgments

>>>>>>>>>>>>>

It HAS LONG been my dream to write a book that would allow me to share part of myself in order to reach out to others and to help them find their way to a better life. It has been soothing to my soul to write this book, and I hope it has the same effect on those who read it.

I want to thank Wes Smith, the writer who assisted me with this book. He is a true professional and he has a great spirit. His contributions went beyond helping me put words on paper. With compassion and understanding, he helped me sort through my thoughts and feelings. I look forward to future projects together.

I want to acknowledge also my daughter, Wendy, whose achievements have made me proud. She is special. My mother, too, has been there for me and for all of my family. I thank her and my brothers and sisters. I love you all. To my nephew Julius, I will always be there for you.

And to those who read this book, I want to thank you and encourage you never to give up, no matter what. We are all capable of making mistakes. We also have the ability to overcome those mistakes and build value in our lives. You can make it happen!

*I dedicate this book to my father, who died in the past year. Through his example, he gave me the strength to find my way. He lived by the scripture from Matthew 8:13, "Enter ye at the strait gate: For wide is the gate and broad is the way that leadeth to destruction, and many there be which go in thereat." With my father's death, the torch of responsibility for my family has passed to me. I accept that responsibility. Rest in peace, Dad. I will do my best.*

*I also dedicate this book to Oprah. Without her influence and her belief in me, I doubt that I ever would have discovered true freedom and what it means. Her knowledge and understanding of the world has added so much to my life. I shall always be grateful to her for helping to fill the hole in my heart. Let the journey continue.*

# Contents

FOREWORD BY STEPHEN R. COVEY      11

CHAPTER 1:    **THE SUCCESS PROCESS**      17

*Taking the Leap to Proactivity*      21
*Acting Upon a Greater Vision*      25
*Taking Life On*      27
*Creating Your Circles of Success*      28
*Climbing the Steps to a Better Life*      33

| | |
|---|---|
| STEP 1: CHECK YOUR ID | 34 |
| STEP 2: CREATE YOUR VISION | 35 |
| STEP 3: DEVELOP YOUR TRAVEL PLAN | 35 |
| STEP 4: MASTER THE RULES OF THE ROAD | 33 |
| STEP 5: STEP INTO THE OUTER LIMITS | 35 |
| STEP 6: PILOT THE SEASONS OF CHANGE | 36 |
| STEP 7: BUILD YOUR DREAM TEAM | 36 |
| STEP 8: WIN BY A DECISION | 36 |
| STEP 9: COMMIT TO YOUR VISION | 37 |

*Living an Honorable and Fulfilling Life*      37

## CHAPTER 2:    **CHECK YOUR ID**                                    **41**

*Validating Your ID*                                              42
*Picking Up the Burden*                                           43
*Self-Knowledge Is Where Success Begins*                          45
*Being a Star Based on Who You Are*                               49
*Digging Deep to Heal the Pain*                                   54
*Confidence, Competence, and Capability*                          55
*Self-Examination and Self-Renewal*                               57
*Checking Your Own ID*                                            60


## CHAPTER 3: **CREATE YOUR VISION**                                  **63**

*Limited Vision, Limited Lives*                                   65
*Deciding Where You Want to Go*                                   66
*Creating a Vision for a Better Life*                             69

| STEP 1: TAKE INVENTORY | 69 |
| STEP 2: TAP INTO YOUR IMAGINATION | 72 |
| STEP 3: SET GOALS | 75 |
| STEP 4: FIND GUIDES AS YOU GO | 83 |
| STEP 5: PUT ON YOUR BLINDERS | 86 |
| STEP 6: ENJOY THE JOURNEY | 87 |


## CHAPTER 4: **DEVELOP YOUR TRAVEL PLAN**                            **91**

*Choosing Action Steps Toward Your Goals*                         93
*Getting on Schedule*                                            100
*Gaining Strength by the Week*                                   101
*Needing No Walls*                                               103
*Mustering a Week's Worth of Willpower*                          105
*Staying Focused on Your Dreams*                                 106
*Preparing Yourself for the Success Process*                     108

CHAPTER 5: **MASTER THE RULES OF THE ROAD**    111

*Packing for Your Journey to a Better Life*    113
*Determination Overcomes Adversity*    114
*Realizing All Things Are Connected*    123
*Checking Your Gear*    124
*Engaging Your Rules of the Road*    127
*Your Rules of the Road*    131
*Fulfilling Responsibilities on the Road*    134


CHAPTER 6: **STEP INTO THE OUTER LIMITS**    137

*Pushing Yourself and Your Talents to the Outer Limits*    139
*Getting Unstuck*    141
*The Risky Business of Life*    143
*Trying Too Hard*    153
*Your Risk-Taking Profile*    155
*Risk Management*    156
*Calculating Risks*    157
*Look Before You Leap*    159
*The Slide for Life*    161


CHAPTER 7: **PILOT THE SEASONS OF CHANGE**    165

*Summoning the Power to Change*    166
*Controlling Your Anger*    169
*Changing for the Good*    171
*Two Types of Change*    173
*Viewing the Process of Change*    177
*Navigating the Seasons of Change*    178
*Developing Patience Is the Key*    189
*Managing the Stress of Change*    190

CHAPTER 8: **BUILD YOUR DREAM TEAM**                193

*It Takes a Team to Produce a Winner*                194
*Being a Part of a Team*                             196
*Teamwork Is a Part of Our Heritage*                 198
*Building Trust*                                     199
*Walking the Walk*                                   204
*Forging Positive Partnerships*                      207
*Communicating with Your Support Team*               213
*Growing Your Support Team*                          216


CHAPTER 9: **WIN BY A DECISION**                     219

*Decisions, Decisions, Decisions*                    221
*Making Good Decisions a Habit*                      230
*Using Your Mind and Your Heart*                     235


CHAPTER 10: **COMMIT TO YOUR VISION**                247

*Committing to Bettering Your Life*                  249
*Honoring Your Commitments*                          256

# Foreword

BY STEPHEN R. COVEY

THE BEST WAY to predict your future is to create it. This staggering idea is embodied in this book and in its remarkable author. I feel honored to write the introduction for my friend and leadership development colleague Stedman Graham. I have tremendous admiration for him and for the mission he has chosen. He not only lives the message presented in this book, but he is a powerful example of someone who has actually made it happen. I also know how genuine, deeply genuine, Stedman is about helping people achieve their highest potential for success.

Stedman Graham cares about the individual. He illustrates how someone's vision can have greater impact than his baggage, for Stedman has not allowed the challenges of his past circumstances to dictate his future. This book's important message is to live out of your imagination and not your history—to hold a vision of the possibility of a better life for you and yours—and to take responsibility and exercise the faith and power you have within you to create that better life. Stedman is an important spokesperson for this message because, in addition to the traditional credentials of advanced educational degrees and significant national leadership positions, he brings the "street" credibility of having faced and conquered the challenges of which he speaks firsthand. Men and women, boys and girls, of all cultures and circumstances throughout the world can take heart in his example. He is a rare mentor who walks his talk.

As you read this book, you will discover early on that Stedman, like many, was born into a host of troubling circumstances and emotional hardships that could have easily left him a bitter and resentful victim. How many of us would be able to sing a similar tune when uncontrollable conditions threaten to kill our hopes and dreams. It becomes easy to excuse our failures and get into a blaming mode, condemning most everything around us. We may seek out friends, or even "experts," who would agree and give us more ammunition to justify our plight, as we proceed to attribute every mistake and misfortune in our lives to poor environment, disturbed upbringing, or genetics. We then sink deeper and deeper into the quicksand of self-pity. Some of us might have had a father who deserted us when we were young, or an uncle who viciously abused us. Perhaps we continually had to scratch and scrape together whatever we could to survive in the face of grinding poverty. Each one of us has a story to tell—a story that is very real. In fact, such injustices and dehumanizing experiences do take their toll, sometimes a *tremendous* toll, in our lives and influence our futures. Yet, the difference between being influenced by and determined by is 180 degrees. The point becomes whether or not you will allow yourself to remain victimized for the rest of your life. This book teaches you how to refuse to let that happen and how your consciousness can eventually produce your reality, rather than letting a harsh reality create your consciousness. In other words, your head creates your world and you stop becoming a victim only when you so choose. It's not the bite of the snake that kills, it's chasing the snake that drives the poison to the heart.

Stedman became a champion and a hero when he refused to let his past direct his future, and he actively took control of his life and became responsible for his own choices and attitudes. This book shows us how to create our own futures, because it is written by a man who has done it in his own life. The voice and tone of this work is positive and hopeful. In the often depressing negativism surrounding us today, hope is an absolute imperative. Otherwise, we become part of the problem, not the solution.

Stedman reaches out to those in conflict not as one who sees himself above them, but as one who has found the way up and out of the often bitter and lonely world of pain, guilt, and prejudice, and as one who wants to help lift others. His Athletes Against Drugs organization is just such an example. To counter the destructive influences of drugs, violence, and crime, Stedman has created an alternative culture of sports programs, education, and mentoring for youth. He becomes a lighthouse to many wishing to avoid the sharp and jagged rocks awaiting them on a stormy sea. By following his "Nine-Step Plan" for a better life, you will learn not to focus on trying to eliminate the problems plaguing your life, but to create a vision for your future, a vision that will, in return, produce the needed antidote for your difficulties. This book is for today—no prerequisites required, except for the desire to believe it can happen and the work ethic to follow your plan.

Stedman is a transition person who teaches us all to become transition people—that is, those who stop the transmission of unhealthy practices, attitudes, and tendencies from one generation to another. By far our greatest legacy is our posterity. What more noble motivation is there than to realize we're doing whatever it takes, including deep sacrifices, for our children and our grandchildren.

In breaking any unhealthy spiral, let us be inspired by what Gandhi taught, "We must become the change we seek in the world."

# You Can
# Make It Happen

*Chapter 1*

# The Success Process

Success is the result of perfection, hard work, learning from failure, loyalty and persistence.

RET. U.S. GEN. COLIN POWELL

EVEN THOUGH YOU may feel as though you already know me, I would like to introduce myself to you. I am Stedman Graham, a native of Whitesboro, New Jersey, an all-black community founded by my ancestor the legendary former U.S. Congressman George H. White. I am the third of six children—the second son—and the only member of my family to complete college. I graduated with a degree in social work from Hardin-Simmons University, where I was co-captain and one of the top scorers on the basketball team.

After college, I served three and a half years in the U.S. Army, most of them in Germany, where I played on both a military basketball team and a team in the European professional basketball league. While in the military service, I earned a master's degree in education, and after fulfilling my service, I worked my way up through the federal department of corrections from a guard in a Colorado prison to the director of education at the U.S. Metropolitan Correctional Center in Chicago.

Although I was on track to perhaps one day become a warden in the federal corrections system, I realized there were other opportunities that appealed to me more, particularly in the rapidly growing field of sports event marketing. I am now chairman and CEO of SGA Incorporated, a management, marketing, and consulting firm specializing in sports, entertainment, and minority markets.

I am also founder of Athletes Against Drugs, a national organization that provides positive role models for young people. In addition, I am a columnist for *Inside Sport* magazine and coauthor of *The Ultimate Guide to Sports Event Management and Marketing*. I serve on the boards of the National Urban League, National Junior Achievement, and Chicago's Jane Addams Hull House social service agency.

And yes, for the last nine years I have been involved in a relationship with one of the most extraordinary and famous women in the world. Earlier, I noted that you may feel as if you know me because you are probably aware of my relationship with Oprah Winfrey. If that relationship is your *only* measure of me, you don't really know me at all, of course. None of us are defined simply by our relationships, nor are we defined by how other people perceive us. It is up to each one of us to define ourselves, and that is a life's work.

Like many people, I wasted a great deal of my life worrying about what others thought of me and how they perceived me. I still struggle with that, even though I have come to realize that it does not matter what others may think of you; what matters most is how you feel about yourself, and that you believe in the *possibilities* for your life. After years of struggling with anger and insecurities that I will detail later, I have come to understand that when you have a sense of your own identity and a vision of where you want to go in your life, you then have the basis for reaching out to the world and going after your dreams for a better life. And *that* is what this book is all about.

In my experiences growing up in New Jersey, serving overseas in the military, working in the federal prison system, and traveling around the country for business or as part of my charity work, I have been exposed to people of all types. I have been struck time and time again by the fact that so many people are struggling to find a way to a better life, a pathway or a method to establish a more meaningful existence in this often daunting world.

It appears to me that so many are struggling because they have no plan, no process for bettering their lives. They just take life as it comes, or they go along and get along until one day it suddenly dawns on them: *My life is out of control. I can't decide what I want to do. I don't have any talents. I'm stuck!* These are the laments of those who have found no meaningful purpose for themselves, and as a result they are unable to get ahead in life, unable to do the things they want to do and enjoy the things they want to enjoy.

I am not referring simply to material things, although financial security is certainly a goal for most of us. It is often said that every day the distinction between the *haves* and the *have-nots* grows greater in the United States. The rich get richer, the poor get poorer. I believe that it does not have to be that way, that *there is enough for all*, that a better life is within reach for each and every one of us if only the have-nots can be taught how the haves did it.

In fact, I believe that it is the absolute right of every man, woman, and child in this country to continuously strive for a better life for themselves and for those around them. I know it may sound naive, but what a nation we would have if that was how each of us led our lives. Think of what might happen if each parent and each child and each family and each community embraced the possibilities for a better life rather than wallowing in their circumstances and blaming the things they believe may be holding them back.

Certainly, these are challenging times. I don't need to tell you that, and I am not going to provide yet another litany here of all that is ailing this country. I do not want to join the doomsayers who are forever providing us with more proof of how hard we have it. My point is that this country is never going to get any better if all we do is blame one another for our problems. What if all those who complain of being victims of poverty, racism, elitism, or their childhoods decided instead to focus on pursuing a better life? What if they took responsibility for their own happiness and success?

How do you do that? How do you find the way to a better life? That is a question I struggled with for a good part of my life. Like so many others, I grew up unaware that there could be a *process* for pursuing success. Oh, I took the usual classes in grade school and high school and college. I learned the basics about mathematics, history, literature, language, geography, government, and other fields, but I entered adulthood without a real plan for my life, and without even any guidelines for *designing* a plan for my life. As a result, for a long time I was without direction. I just took life as it came, rather than taking my life where I wanted it to go.

Believe it or not, part of my problem was that I had done fairly well in life without a plan. I'd gotten an education, traveled extensively, and I'd had good jobs. I am not saying that I was the most successful guy in the world; in fact, like you, I am still trying to get my piece of the pie. But the difference today is that *now* I have a plan and a process for going after what I want.

A few years ago, it dawned on me that although I was doing okay, I was like a guy on a runaway wagon. I was moving, but I didn't have any control over where I was going. I was a passenger, rather than a driver, in my own life. For a number of reasons, which I will detail later in this book, I struggled for many years with feelings of inadequacy and unworthiness. The reasons don't matter all that much. Most people have to deal with some sort of baggage weighing them down, whether it be racism, sexism, a physical deformity or mental disability, a background of poverty, or an abusive relationship. What does matter is that we learn to see beyond those things, and to envision a better life so that we can pursue it.

I guarantee you, there is a great possibility that you can better your life. It's said that the average person generally develops only about 2 percent of his or her potential. That means that 98 percent of your gifts go unopened or untapped. That leaves plenty of room for bettering yourself.

For me, there came a point when I finally understood that there was more out in the world for me. One thing that triggered this awakening was my increasing exposure, relatively recently in my life, to people who did seem to be in control of their own destinies. These people were from varied backgrounds and many different parts of the country, but they all seemed to have one thing in common: they understood that there is a *process for pursuing success*. Whether they did it instinctively or it was taught to them, nearly every successful person I know has followed this process or one very similar to it. In actively pursuing a better life, they do not drift along. They do not let events or others rule their lives. They have become the most active and influential force in their own lives. They are what my friend and mentor Stephen Covey describes as *proactive* people.

## TAKING THE LEAP TO PROACTIVITY

Another friend of mine, Julius W. Erving II, is such a person. You may know him as "Dr. J," one of the all-time greatest scorers in professional basketball and now a television sports analyst for NBC. "Doc," as I call him, is also a very successful businessman with a highly diversified portfolio that includes co-ownership of the Philadelphia Coca-Cola Bottling Co. and a seat on the board of directors of Converse. It's been written that more than anyone else, including Michael Jordan, Doc made the NBA what it is to-

day. But sportswriters and fans often forget that early in his athletic career, Doc had to fight to get recognition. In spite of his
incredible athletic gifts, nothing was handed him. He was, in
fact, a late bloomer in the sport. In high school, he was only six
feet, three inches tall as a senior and although he had obvious talent, he was passed over by the major powers of college basketball. As a man who has never allowed his circumstances to hold
him back, Julius Erving played much taller than his height.
Looking back, he says his relatively small stature early in his
playing career was a blessing: "It prohibited me from ever taking
anything for granted. It made me have realistic expectations, focus on my studies first, and have a more balanced approached to
life and the realization that basketball is a game."

Instead of going to a major basketball power, Doc played two
seasons at the University of Massachusetts, where he grew three
and a half inches. Although he was forced to play center, which
was not his natural position, he averaged 27 points and 19
rebounds in his junior year. He left school then, lured by the opportunity to make a living playing the sport he loves, and a four-
year, $500,000 contract. He began his pro career not in the NBA,
but in the fledgling ABA Virginia Squires, in 1971. Two seasons
later, he was that league's Most Valuable Player, an award he
won again in 1975, sharing it with George McGinnis, and once
more in 1976 while leading the New York Nets to the ABA cham-
pionship.

In 1976, the ABA merged with the NBA, and Dr. J was traded
to the Philadelphia 76ers, where he became the premier player in
the expanded professional basketball league. Like Michael Jordan today, Julius had incredible leaping ability, agility, and
quickness for a big man. Known for soaring over his opponents,
he was as big a draw around the league as Jordan is today.

What I admire about him the most, however, is not so much
his athletic skills and accomplishments as the strength of his
character. The head of the NBA, David Stern, once said, "He set

a new standard for the way the players were encouraged to be-have with the media, with fans, with family values. Dr. J made it cool to have great values and to flaunt those values and to demonstrate them." When my friend was inducted into the NBA Hall of Fame in 1993, he showed that character when he offered his thoughts on his legacy. "I want the youngsters to understand anything you work toward in a positive direction can happen," he said. "I'm not just talking athletics. I'm talking education, pol-itics . . . whatever level."

For so many young people, and others too, who find them-selves under siege by crime, violence, drugs, physical abuse, and other negative factors, it is difficult to believe that there is a way out. Doc didn't worry about the negative factors in his life; he fo-cused on the possibilities and took control of his own destiny. We need more of that sort of thinking today. Increasingly, the streets of our cities and even our suburban communities are afflicted with gangs and crime and drugs and violence. We all are under assault by outside forces that would deter us from our pursuit of better lives for ourselves and our loved ones.

Young people in particular feel threatened and uncertain of where their futures are headed. A recent study among Virginia high school students found that more than one in four had car-ried a gun, knife, or other weapon into school at least once. One of every three New York City high school students said they feel physically threatened during the school year. Almost half of them claim to have carried a weapon into class. Not long ago, seven hundred weapons were found in and around the public schools in Philadelphia. It is no wonder that two times as many teenagers as adults die of murder, or that three times as many teenagers as adults kill themselves. It is not surprising either that at least 17 percent of America's teachers live in fear of violent at-tack. The *Washington Post* has editorialized about this breakdown in our society: "While the severity of actions ranges from simple cheating at school, to pushing drugs, to cold-blooded murder . . .

the depth of the problem has reached a point where common decency can no longer be described as common. Somewhere, somehow . . . the traditional value system got disconnected for a disturbing number of America's new generation."

According to a recent *Newsweek* article, the nation's welfare rolls have soared to record levels. Nearly one in seven Americans is receiving payments from government programs for families with dependent children, yet only about 11 percent of the 4.6 million parents who take that money participate in any of the accompanying programs for education, training, or job search programs. The stubborn fact is that many of those who are most dependent on public assistance are unable to get and keep full-time jobs in either the public or private sector, and even the best work and training programs barely dent the relief roles.

An environment of fear nurtures only more fear and violence and tragedy unless the people trapped within it can see something better for their lives.

People who consider themselves "victims" of their circumstances will always remain victims unless they develop a greater vision for their lives. They never came to see, as Julius Erving and other successful people have, that a better life is possible for anyone willing to pursue it. We can't all be professional athletes or television stars, of course. But each of us has the ability to lead a dynamic life by pursuing our own unique goals and dreams. The poorest of us, the weakest, the least popular has the power within to pursue a better life. The greatest difficulty, however, is learning to believe that it is possible for you to achieve your dreams and then to commit to achieving those dreams.

Do you believe that you can be an active force in your own life? That you can seize control? Do you have goals that you are motivated to pursue? Do you continually strive for a better life so that once you have reached a goal you immediately look for another? Are you chasing your dreams, or putting in your time? People who let events and circumstances dictate their lives are living *reactively*. That means that they don't act *on* life, they only react *to* it.

## ACTING UPON A GREATER VISION

Reactive people do not take responsibility for their own lives and their own feelings. They feel good about themselves only if other people say nice things to them. On the other hand, if someone says something bad to them, or criticizes them, they let it affect their view of themselves. Too often, people like this are dominated by how they feel rather than what they think. Those people who are actively controlling their own lives, on the other hand, are driven by what they value: their goals and the principles for living their lives that they have selected after careful thought. They understand that what happens *to* them is not nearly as important as how they choose to react to it.

I have a favorite book, a tiny book that fits in the palm of my hand, that I often send to people. It is called *As a Man Thinketh* and it was written by the philosopher James Allen, who believed that "as a man thinketh in his heart, he is." Allen believed that people's thoughts drive their actions, that their perceptions of themselves make them who they are. His book begins with this little poem: "Mind is the master power that molds and makes. And man is mind and evermore he takes the tool of thought, and, shaping what he wills, brings forth a thousand joys, a thousand ills. He thinks in secret, and it comes to pass: Environment is but his looking glass."

The message of that poem is that each of us can control our lives by controlling our thought processes. If we can *envision* a better life for ourselves and our loved ones, then we are on the way to *creating* that life. I read a great example of the power of having a vision of where you want to go in a publication put out by the Covey Leadership Center, operated by Stephen Covey.

In his *7 Habits Report* magazine, a professor from Minnesota, R. Kent Crookston, wrote of his experience as a teenager working in a sash and door factory in Alberta, Canada.

Crookston was assigned to a cabinet shop supervised by Hans, a Romanian craftsman who was in charge of creating the teak woodwork for an entire courtroom for the Royal Canadian Mounted Police. It was a big project involving an expensive wood, and Crookston was given a series of small tasks as part of the project. Unsure of himself, or of how his work fit into the project, Crookston kept making mistakes even though he was trying hard to do the job right.

Finally, Hans pulled him aside and showed him the detailed blueprints for the project. The intricate drawings showed the young worker exactly how his work fit into the greater project. Suddenly, Crookston had a complete vision of what he was supposed to be doing and of how everything was going to fit together. Before, Hans had been giving him instructions only one task at a time. He had little understanding of what the final result was supposed to be, and so he worked tentatively, unsure of himself and unable to make knowledgeable decisions. When he saw the blueprint and the drawings of the completed job, Crookston gained the confidence of someone with a strong vision of where he was headed.

I was reminded of the importance and the power of having a vision for your life during the O. J. Simpson trial, believe it or not. I won't tell you what I thought of the trial or the verdict. Instead, I'd like to focus on one participant who didn't get much attention during the circus that surrounded that trial, even though he may well have been one of the most admirable people involved. You probably don't even remember him. His name is Henry Lee, and he is one of the world's most respected forensic scientists; he testified for Simpson's defense. In a trial marked by witnesses and testimony that made a mockery of the truth, Henry Lee was the one person everyone believed was telling the truth, or at least the truth as he understood it. People feel that way about Henry Lee because of the strength of his character.

A Chinese refugee at the age of seven, he didn't reach the United States until he was a young man with a wife. Here, he worked as a waiter and kung fu instructor to pay his way through school. He is now one of the foremost authorities on the use of DNA in criminal investigations, and he is the director of the Connecticut State Forensics Science Laboratory. Like Dr. J, Henry Lee is another example of what you can accomplish when you know who you are and have faith in what you can do.

It's not easy to pull yourself out of a rut or to overcome hardships and better your life. That is why I recommend you build strong and supportive relationships as you follow the processes detailed in this book. I encourage you to take control of your own life and to focus on pursuing a better life for yourself, but not to isolate yourself in the process. That is one problem I have with many so-called *self-help* books—they sometimes encourage the reader to be self-*obsessed*. Isolating yourself is not healthy spiritually, mentally, or physically, and it is certainly not the way to achieve a better life. I believe nobody makes it alone. So, as you follow the processes and steps described and recommended in this book, always keep in mind your relationships. Nurture them, build them, and lean on them when you need to. Do not be afraid to ask for help or encouragement along the way. Remember also that just as you need a hand now and then, so do those coming behind you.

## TAKING LIFE ON

By simply making the decision to read this book, you have taken a step toward asserting control over your life. You have obviously decided you are no longer going to allow outside influence to dictate how you live your life. That is a sign of a person who is actively engaged in life. Think about the people you know and work with. Can you think of one who appears to fit the description of someone who is *actively engaged* in life? If you can, I'll bet I can describe that person for you. (I'll describe the person as a woman but it could be a man too, of course.) I'll wager that this person you are thinking of is known as someone who can always be relied upon to get the job done. She is known for finding solutions where others may only see problems. She is often asked to head committees or to organize events. She is almost always on time and looks good whether in a sweatsuit or evening wear. This is a woman who almost never says, *I can't, If only*, or *I would do that but* . . . Instead, this woman uses positive, active language such as *I can, I will*, or *Let's find a way to make this work*. Did I describe the characteristics and manner of the person you were thinking of? These people are easy to spot in any situation because they are usually in positions of leadership. They are the ones with the signs on their desks that say, *Lead, Follow, or Get Out of the Way!*

People who control their own lives are like those cities of the future you have seen with huge bubbles covering them. Like those futuristic cities, these people are self-contained. It doesn't matter what goes on around them, they are in control. There may be chaos in the surrounding universe. They may be under bombardment from exterior forces. But they are protected from it all by their bubble of self-assurance and self-control. They do not worry about things they cannot control outside their bubble; they focus instead on matters within their power to influence.

## CREATING YOUR CIRCLES OF SUCCESS

These self-controlled people understand that we cannot do much about outside forces such as the things other people may say about us or the perceptions they have of us. We can only focus on those things that are within our bubbles, or what I call our *Success Circles.* The things that matter most to me and that I have the power to influence are inside my Success Circles.

For purposes of this book, let's consider three circles labeled *relationships*, *job or career*, and *community*. These are the primary areas in which you can seek to create a better life for yourself and to generate success.

Your relationships include family, spouse or partner, friends, and all others who are close to you. This is perhaps the most critical area, for without consistent and strong relationships, it is difficult to build a meaningful life. A person may have a great career and success in the community, but without friends and family and loved ones, those things may not be enough. A life without strong mutually supportive relationships can be a hollow existence.

Having a rewarding job or career is also highly important in building a better life for yourself. We all need something to give our lives structure, and a job or career does that. Now, I include in this category the career of being a full-time and part-time parent, which is certainly one of the most important jobs around, and it also without a doubt gives structure to a life, as any parent who has had to follow a schedule of piano lessons, soccer or baseball practice, and school events knows all too well.

The third category, of community, is one that I give a very broad definition to. We all need to have meaningful relationships and also work that challenges us and provides structure for our lives. I believe we also need to connect to a community of some sort. Your community can include your neighborhood, your town, your church, your school district, your county or state. Your role in the community may involve volunteer work, holding an appointed or elected office, working on a neighborhood committee, or participation and involvement in your church. I consider this category to include any role outside the home or office that involves you in the lives of the people and the world around you. We all need to develop a sense of dedication to something greater than ourselves. You can pursue a better life for yourself by working at the same time to better the world around you. In fact, by involving yourself in your community, you may well discover greater opportunities for yourself. I know of a great many people who have networked their way to better lives through their involvement in local, regional, and national groups such as Junior Achievement or the Scouts.

On a sheet of paper, draw three Success Circles, one for each category listed above, and within each one make a list of ten things you can do to better your life, by making changes or improvements in your personal life and relationships, your job or career, or your place in the community. Examples in each category might include *spending more time with a loved one doing things that you both enjoy,* or *getting more training,* or *volunteering to work in a literacy program for young people.*

These three circles of interest are by no means the only ones. Each person could probably come up with a dozen or more, but this book will focus on these three areas because they are generally applicable to everyone and because these three represent key aspects of our lives. I've found that if things are not going well in any one of these areas of your life, chances are it has a negative impact on each of the other areas. That is why it is so important to have a balanced life in which you pay attention to your relationships, your job or career, and the community around you, whether that means your neighbors, your town, your church or congregation, or the region in which you live.

You may develop more specific Success Circles later to include your special interests. Mine include everything from my golf and tennis games to my personal fitness routine. Also, please note that often your circles will overlap. Your relationships may include friends who are also co-workers. If your job is full-time parenting, that will involve a great deal of overlapping between your work and your relationships. If you are a public servant,

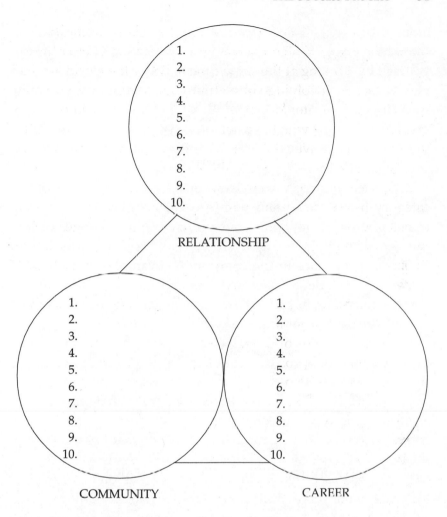

then undoubtedly your career and your community Success Circles will regularly be intertwined. In fact, I believe it benefits you to have these key areas of your life intersect because it strengthens the quality of your life. It gives you a more solid base from which to pursue a better life.

The circles are simply a way of helping you focus on the most important areas of your life when you undertake the *Success*

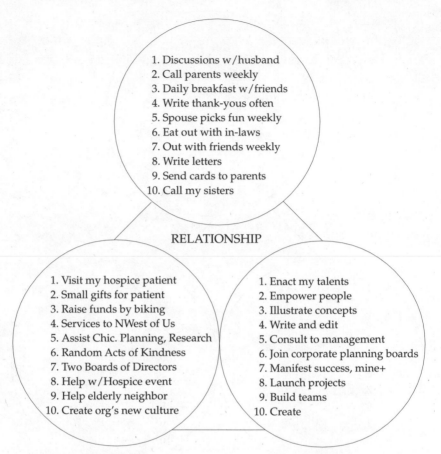

1. Discussions w/husband
2. Call parents weekly
3. Daily breakfast w/friends
4. Write thank-yous often
5. Spouse picks fun weekly
6. Eat out with in-laws
7. Out with friends weekly
8. Write letters
9. Send cards to parents
10. Call my sisters

RELATIONSHIP

1. Visit my hospice patient
2. Small gifts for patient
3. Raise funds by biking
4. Services to NWest of Us
5. Assist Chic. Planning, Research
6. Random Acts of Kindness
7. Two Boards of Directors
8. Help w/Hospice event
9. Help elderly neighbor
10. Create org's new culture

1. Enact my talents
2. Empower people
3. Illustrate concepts
4. Write and edit
5. Consult to management
6. Join corporate planning boards
7. Manifest success, mine+
8. Launch projects
9. Build teams
10. Create

COMMUNITY                      CAREER

*Process.* People who are in control of their lives have that sort of focus, and because of it they are always seeking to expand their influence and to grow and seek to better their lives.

Reactive people, on the other hand, tend to focus on things outside their control. They tend to blame others for what happens to them, and to always assume the role of victim. Because of the lack of control of their lives, they have difficulty pursuing success even if they are given a process, because they have relinquished responsibility for what happens to them.

In truth, you must take responsibility for yourself if you are going to pursue success and a better life in this world. Now I'm going to give up a secret about this process for pursuing success: *It's not complicated.* Some people would have you believe it is extremely difficult, and that you'd better pay them a lot of money to help you understand it. The truth is, the Success Process has been around for thousands of years. You can find elements of it in the writings of ancient philosophers such as Plato (*The life which is unexamined is not worth living*) and Aristotle (*With regard to excellence, it is not enough to know, but we must try to have and use it*), in the Bible (*Be strong and of good courage, be not afraid, neither be thou dismayed: for the Lord thy God is with thee whithersoever though goest*), in Shakespeare (*This above all: to thine own self be true, And it must follow, as the night the day, Thou canst not then be false to any man*), and in self-help and motivational books dating from the turn of the century to the modern day.

## CLIMBING THE STEPS TO A BETTER LIFE

You can also see this Success Process being lived all around you by successful people ranging from athletes to civil rights and civic leaders to business giants and celebrities. I see it in the lives of some of my closest friends. Based on my study of a wide range of successful people, some of whom I know personally, I have formulated for you the *Nine-Step Plan for Success* program. It is designed to help you get on track to a better life as it relates to your family or personal relationships, your job or career, and your role as a positive force in your community. These steps are not miracle cures, nor are they guarantees of wealth, fame, and eternal happiness. They are merely steps to get you on track to better yourself, whether you are just entering the workplace out of high school or college, eager to move up in the corporate world, looking to start your own business, or simply wanting to revitalize your life.

As you follow these steps, you will probably learn a lot about yourself. You may even discover, as I did, that the biggest obstacles blocking your pursuit of a better life are those that you unconsciously put in your own path: past hurts and negative attitudes that hold you back, a poor self-image, the notion that you are somehow a *victim* of life rather than a life *force*. By helping you to better understand yourself, by showing you how to take control, these steps can free you to pursue your vision for a better life.

Consider these steps guidelines and reminders to keep you focused and on track in your quest for a more satisfying and rewarding job, a more balanced personal life, and a meaningful role in your community. If this book serves that simple purpose, it should be invaluable to you. Read each of the steps carefully, do the exercises that accompany them, and, most important, think seriously about how each of them can be applied to your pursuit of a better life.

Here is a brief summary of my Nine-Step Plan for Success, which will be explored in depth throughout the rest of the book.

## 1.  CHECK YOUR ID

Before you can decide what you want for your life, you first must understand who you are, what the influences are on your life, why you act and think the way you do. Some describe this as searching for *self-awareness*. I call it *checking your ID*. Before you take off on any serious journey these days, you must first make sure that you have valid identification with you. The same holds true for your journey on the Success Process.

## 2. CREATE YOUR VISION

To seek a better life, you first have to decide what you want for your life. This involves exploring the possibilities for your life through your dreams and aspirations; evaluating the unique characteristics, talents, and skills you bring to the table; and then setting ambitious but realistic goals for your family and personal relationships, your job or career, and your role in your community.

## 3. DEVELOP YOUR TRAVEL PLAN

Once you have established your goals, you need a plan to pursue your vision. In this step, I will help you develop a plan that takes into consideration each area of your life. I will also show you how to chart the best path by using the values that make up your belief system as your markers.

## 4. MASTER THE RULES OF THE ROAD

Every day you will encounter distractions that might prevent you from working toward your goal, or at the very least, slow you down in your journey. In this chapter, I will teach you how to persevere and keep on keeping on. I will provide keys to self-motivation so that you will have the strength not to be easily distracted or defeated.

## 5. STEP INTO THE OUTER LIMITS

There are always risks when you chase after a dream because growth requires that you leave your comfort zone and enter unknown territory. But without confronting those risks and facing your fears, you'll never, as Nike says, "Just do it." Now, the truth is, you may fail in some of your efforts, but you will never succeed if you are not willing to risk failure. And even if you do fail, you can learn from the experience and try again. To do that, you will need courage, and you will also need to have faith in your ability to achieve your goals.

## 6. PILOT THE SEASONS OF CHANGE

Many people never go after their dreams for a better life because they are afraid of change. The fact is that most of the time you cannot move ahead without leaving something behind. If you are not getting what you want out of life, you have to change your approach to it. To get what you want, you have to become the person who deserves it. And that means changing attitudes, maybe even changing important parts of your life. To embrace change you have to view it as a natural process in your life, and in this step I will teach you how to manage change by being resilient, and I will teach you patience so that you learn to give yourself an adequate amount of time to accept change and adjust successfully to it.

## 7. BUILD YOUR DREAM TEAM

To pursue success effectively, you must build supportive relationships that will help you work toward your goals. To build those relationships, you need to learn to trust others; and to earn their trust, you in turn must learn to be trustworthy.

## 8. WIN BY A DECISION

Making decisions wisely is one of your greatest challenges. This involves assessing your personal strengths, needs, and resources, but also checking them against your belief system, and then evaluating your choices based on that assessment. You need a strong heart and a wise mind to do that, and in this chapter, I will help you develop thoughtfulness in your decision-making.

## 9. COMMIT TO YOUR VISION

In this step, I will review all of the previous material with you, and then teach you how to make a true commitment to achieving your vision for a successful life. You can set all the goals and make all the plans in the world, but unless you truly commit yourself to going after them, you'll never achieve them. Having a commitment involves pledging your time and energy to the pursuit of your vision, and making that pursuit a top priority in your life. To do that, you have to be committed.

## LIVING AN HONORABLE AND FULFILLING LIFE

When I think about commitment, I think of my father, whose primary commitment in life was to his family. As I was working on this book, a very sad thing happened. My father, Stedman Graham Sr., died after a long illness. Dad was a shy and humble working-class guy, a house painter. He had a limited vision for his life, but it was an honorable one. He wanted to provide for his family through hard work. He did that. He lived a decent and productive life. He took care of his wife and children and we respected him for that. He gave me a sense of determination and perseverance and honesty as well as the ability to keep going in spite of difficulties. If he started something, he stuck with it until the end. He was a very strong man, and I like to think I have inherited some of his strength of character.

Oprah believes that when someone close to you dies, you take on some of that person's strength and spirit. I think she is right. When my father died, I was struck with this sense of commitment and responsibility toward my family. I felt I had to carry on as the leader for my mother and my sisters and brothers. I asked myself, *How can I best serve them and make their lives easier?* At his funeral, I promised Dad's departed spirit that I would take over for him and look after everyone. I also promised that I would make him proud of me by going after my dreams and goals. In his own quiet way, he served many people. I promised that I would carry on his spirit of serving and encouraging others to be their best. That is why I have dedicated this book to his memory.

Each of the following chapters is devoted to one of the nine steps, offering exercises to help you grasp the principle and virtue that is the focus of each step. It also has valuable, practical instruction that can help you change your life for the better, and particularly to help you realize that you are not defined by your circumstances; it is your vision of the *possibilities* that matters most.

What does that mean? Ask the eight children of Carrie B. Ponder, a single mother in the inner city of Chicago, where street gangs, crime, drugs, and violence are circumstances that too often steal the lives of young people away from their parents. But Mrs. Ponder had a vision for her children, and she taught them that vision. She taught them to look beyond the graffiti that covered their neighborhood like the kudzu vines that smother the countryside in Ponder's native Mississippi. Carrie Ponder taught her children as her grandparents back in Mississippi had taught her, that *you use what you need to succeed.* I know, because two of her sons are friends of mine and I have become an admirer of their dynamic family.

Mrs. Ponder, who separated from her husband when their youngest child was still a toddler, was determined to use every tool within her grasp to make her children aware of the greater possibilities for their lives. As she was raising them, she worked mostly in their schools to be close to them, monitoring their progress. She did not earn enough to feed their bodies so she relied on food stamps. To nourish their intellects, she mined every resource available.

She enrolled them in youth centers, church organizations, and library programs. She scavenged on weekends for cheap tickets to plays, museums, and the opera. "When there was very little money, I would just pack a lunch and go to a park and sit around the Art Institute," she once told a *Chicago Tribune* reporter. "Sometimes we would just ride on a bus from one end of the city to the other and talk about architecture."

Breakfast table discussions for these children were centered on the events they'd seen broadcast on the evening news the night before. "She wanted to broaden us so that we would have a large perspective," Erik Ponder said of his mother.

The Ponder children were taught to see beyond their circumstances even when the family was forced out of the cramped three-bedroom apartment where they had lived for ten years. Finding a new home for eight children was a daunting challenge, but Mrs. Ponder was determined to keep her family out of the city's crime-ridden public housing projects. The alternatives were not much better, however. She found an apartment in one of the worst neighborhoods in the inner city, but a week after they had moved in, the building burned down, destroying most of their possessions.

Mrs. Ponder did not let even those circumstances destroy her vision of a better life for her children. "To find everything you own is gone is devastating. But the children were still healthy. I forgot about the loss of material things. We had to do a comeback," she told the *Tribune*.

She found another apartment for her family and returned to her life's mission: to show her children that they were not bound by their circumstances as long as they believed in the possibility of a better life. A few years ago, the Chicago mother and her grown children were gathered together for a ceremony put on by the Chicago Youth Centers in honor of Mrs. Ponder for her com-

mitment and perseverance in pursuing her vision of a better life
for her children.

With her were her sons and daughters, all of them either in college or graduates of universities such as Princeton, the University of Chicago, Northwestern University, and the University of
Pennsylvania. Her youngest, Tracie, was not present because she
was performing with the Alvin Ailey American Dance Theatre in
New York. But the others were all there: Rhinold, a lawyer; Regi-
nald, an advertising executive; Erik, a doctoral student in politi-
cal science; Sharon, a teacher; Maria, just graduated from college;
Angela and Alvina, who were both still in college.

"The bottom line is that we were taught not to view our circumstances negatively," Rhinold said. "Though poor of pocket,
we were not poor of mind and spirit."

Unless we learn to look beyond what has happened to us, and
to take control of our lives, we will never rise above. In the following pages, I hope to instill in you at least some of the courageous spirit and hope that Mrs. Ponder passed on to her
children. As you read, put your circumstances out of your mind,
consider only the *possibilities* for bettering your life.

## Chapter 2
# Check Your ID

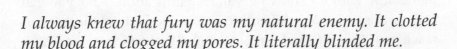

*I always knew that fury was my natural enemy. It clotted my blood and clogged my pores. It literally blinded me.*

MAYA ANGELOU

NOT TOO LONG AGO, I was walking on Michigan Avenue in Chicago when a construction worker, who was crossing the street with me, said, "Hey, Oprah's boyfriend, how's it going?"

There was a time when I might have ignored the guy or given him a cold stare for calling me that. But instead, I reached out, shook his hand, and began talking with him. We walked across the street together and continued our conversation on the street corner. I can't remember all that was said. But I do remember this. By the end of the conversation, he wasn't calling me "Oprah's boyfriend" anymore. He was calling me "Mr. Graham."

That construction worker had no idea how long it took me to learn to handle situations like that gracefully. For a long time, it chewed me up when people treated me as nothing more than *Oprah's boyfriend*. But as I developed the Success Process that is the heart of this book, I learned not only how to deal with people who don't really know me, I learned to know myself.

I no longer feel that I have to prove myself, but it wasn't so long ago that I was a victim of my own mistaken identity, and my lack of self-knowledge and self-understanding hindered my ability to pursue a better life.

## VALIDATING YOUR ID

You can't open a bank account, drive a car, or even get on an airplane now without showing valid identification. And you can believe this, it is very difficult to get on the path of success and reach your full potential unless you also first validate your identity by deciding exactly who you are and where you want to go. Achieving *self-awareness*, then, is the first, and perhaps one of the most important steps in the Success Process.

You have an invalid ID when you don't understand yourself and your actions. *Why did I get so upset over that? Why am I so nervous around her?* You validate your identity when you come to understand yourself. You do that by analyzing what motivates you and controls your emotional behavior and your moods. Once you understand where those attitudes come from and analyze them, then you can begin to understand not only why you act the way you do, but also why others *perceive you* the way they do. This understanding gives you the power to change and control your behavior in a more positive and effective manner. It allows you to develop building blocks and begin the process of acting on the steps you put in each of your Success Circles dealing with your personal relationships, your career, and your community.

The first step in developing fundamental *self-awareness* is to examine the things that influence your behavior, both those that hold you back and those that push you to pursue a better life. This can be a painful process to undergo. It can mean confronting some serious issues and realities in your life. The poet Maya Angelou, who has not had an easy life, once said, "*Success is not fame or fortune. It is picking up that burden and keeping on walking and not letting the pain trip you up."*

## PICKING UP THE BURDEN

Let me tell you how I came to understand and deal with the things that were holding me back. Several years ago, I went down to the corner Walgreen's store in our Chicago neighborhood to get something, and this street person in the store began heckling me: *"Hey, Oprah's boyfriend, give me some money."*

People in the store stopped and stared at me, probably wondering how I was going to react, whether I would get upset or handle it smoothly. It was really embarrassing but I left the store without acknowledging the guy or his comments. Later when I saw Oprah, I told her that it was painful for me to be treated like that. Her response was not particularly sympathetic: "Why would some guy yelling for money be so painful for you?"

She reacted without much sympathy because this was not the first time something like this had happened. We had talked about the impact of her fame on my ego many times, but this time her question got me thinking, *Why did it bother me so much?*

It was embarrassing, sure, but why did the public perception of me as Oprah's boyfriend seem to trigger so much pain and anger? I thought about the roots of that pain and anger for several days and nights, and that reflection took me into some painful suppressed memories that caused me to realize that the hurt was coming from a far deeper source than some stranger in a drugstore.

The problem, I realized, was not his, or Oprah's, it was mine. The truth was that ever since Oprah had become a national celebrity, I'd been increasingly uncomfortable in our relationship. Her fame had thrown the balance off and I didn't know how to restore it. Our relationship had begun at a point in my life when I was just beginning to find my way as a person, and Oprah was just establishing herself in local television. We had been on fairly equal footing. We shared many of the same friends. People treated us like an ordinary couple.

Although in many ways we are different, Oprah and I are similar in some very important respects, and our differences tend to complement each other. I am certainly not as quick-witted as she; she is three steps ahead of me and nearly everyone else on the planet. She is also a far better communicator, no surprise there. I am more conservative than she is, and I tend to stick with things longer than she does. I set rules and follow them, while she goes with the flow. For example, the rule at our meals together is that we don't feed table scraps to our dogs, Solomon and Sophie. Oprah reminds me of that rule all the time, even as she is slipping food to them.

My point is that Oprah and I were pretty much just another couple until she became everyone in the world's best friend and confidante, and then, suddenly, instead of Stedman and Oprah, it became OPRAH! and her boyfriend, the tall guy. I became an unequal partner in the relationship, at least in the eyes of the public. That was difficult for me to handle and I'd wager that many men from traditional families such as mine would have similar problems adjusting. I had to shed some very traditional male attitudes and habits as her fame and her wealth rapidly grew.

I went through some rocky times in learning to cope with all of the attention and occasional trash journalism, but I realize now that Oprah's rise to fame was probably the best thing that could have happened for both of us. It forced me into examining myself and the influences on my life and to confront my private fears and insecurities. As Maya Angelou has written: *"Pressure can change you into something quite precious, quite wonderful, quite beautiful and extremely hard."*

The pressure of dealing with the changes in my relationship

forced me to look deep inside and to strive for greater understanding of myself. That is something we all need to do throughout our lives. You can't understand the world and how you respond to it until you first know yourself. You can't change the things you don't like about yourself until you search out the things that influence you and motivate you and hurt you.

## SELF-KNOWLEDGE IS WHERE SUCCESS BEGINS

*To know yourself is the first, and most important, step in the process of pursuing your dreams and goals.* A key element of validating your own identity, or self-awareness, is becoming secure enough in who you are to accept the influence of others on you. If you aren't secure in yourself, odds are you won't be open to the love, caring, and help of those around you.

I discovered this when I began searching to find out why Oprah's fame and the public response to our relationship was so crippling for me. When I went inward and found the cause of that hurt, I learned a great deal about myself. I began to understand and accept myself to the degree that I became free to create a vision for my life, a better life than I might ever have designed if I hadn't been forced to really look at the influences, good and bad, that determined my actions and my feelings.

That journey, in part, is what inspired me to write this book, so that others too might find their own way. Although people tell me that I appear to be a self-confident person, the truth is that, like many people, I have struggled with insecurity for a great deal of my life. My lack of self-confidence traces back to my youth and my family's circumstances.

We lived in Whitesboro, an African-American community surrounded by a county that was otherwise all white. Our town did not have a lot of amenities, although it was located in a generally affluent resort region of southern New Jersey. Because it was a town of minorities, Whitesboro was often ridiculed. There was one hurtful but untrue phrase in particular that hangs over the town to this day. It claimed that "nothing good ever comes out of Whitesboro." When you hear that sort of talk from your early childhood, it can wear on your self-esteem, and your sense of being able to rise above your circumstances.

Although I have come to disagree with those people who have a "victim" mentality and claim that they can never get ahead because the "system" is against them or "the establishment" won't allow them to break free of the poverty cycle, at one time I thought the same way. African Americans are bombarded with negative images, and sometimes we even bring them down upon each other. In my grade school, which was all black, I was sometimes taunted as "Whitey" by other kids because of my light skin color. Among blacks I felt I had to prove I was as black as anyone else, and among whites I felt I had to prove my worth even more.

Most African Americans have similar stories. The truth is that all people have their own private pain to deal with and work through in their lives. African Americans, however, always have to bear the burden of racism and prejudice in addition to any other challenges in their lives.

On top of that negative racial image, my own family was deeply affected by the learning disabilities of my two youngest brothers, Jimmy and Darry. Back then, they were called "retarded," though now they are described as "developmentally disabled." Today, there are many support groups and counseling programs to help families deal with mental disabilities, but we didn't have access to those services back then. Sadly, our entire family was stigmatized because of public ignorance about mental illness at that time.

There was a great deal of shame cast upon us because of my brothers and their disabilities. Because of that shame, my parents never talked to us about it. When I was a child, I did not understand the family dysfunction that resulted. I want to make it clear that I love my family. Jimmy and Darry, who are now in their mid-thirties, are my favorite two guys in this world. Every time I see them, they warm my heart with their loving affection. I went home to visit them recently and when I got there I was deeply touched by my brothers' love and their warmth. It really touches me when they hug me and show me off to their friends as their big brother.

Now I understand their handicap and my family's response to it. I understand that mental illness is nothing to be ashamed of. I have always felt my brothers are wonderful people, but I have to say that in years past, before I came to grips with their disability, I was aloof toward them. I was standoffish to them because as an adolescent and teenager—those vital years when our self-images are forged—I had been made to feel ashamed of them and my-self.

I was in grade school when my brothers were born, a few years apart, and it took some time for it to dawn on me that they were "different." Around the house, they were just my little brothers, but in the neighborhood, I was never allowed to forget their disability. In school I'd hear, "Your brothers aren't right." I'd defend them, of course, but when I'd go home and tell my parents what others were saying, they told me just to ignore it. They didn't help me handle it because they didn't know how to handle it themselves.

Nobody in my family talked about it. I think my father was particularly affected. He withdrew emotionally and socially from our family, and from the world around him. Aside from his work, he rarely left the house. He was a good, honest, and hard-working man, and although he showed no interest in my athletic achievements, or in my life outside the home, I do not blame him or judge him. I am sure it was just the only way he could find to respond to complex and painful emotions. I never talked to him about it, but I think he felt guilt and shame over having fathered two mentally disabled sons. He withdrew with those feelings, and had little to do with people because of his shame.

But I couldn't hide. I was teased a lot about my brothers and I got into a lot of fights. I was so driven to prove I had value as a person that, if anybody challenged me about anything, or in any way suggested I was full of hot air, they really had a fight on their hands. Along with covering my insecurities by getting upset, I became a perfectionist. I analyzed every situation relentlessly to make sure I made as few mistakes as possible so that I would not embarrass myself.

Now I realize that being a perfectionist inhibits you because if you wait for something to be perfect, you may never get anything done. For a long time, though, I was driven to always be the best—and also to let everyone know it. When I earned All-State honors in basketball, I insisted the high school assistant principal announce it over the public address system. Looking back, I have come to understand that it was my immature way of dealing with my insecurities and the negative image of my family in the community. I was trying to prove that I had value, that I was not limited like my brothers. Sometimes, however, my boasting only made matters worse.

I'll never forget what happened to me one day in Mister T. A.'s, a small coffee shop where teenagers hung out. It was owned by T. A. Richardson, who was a businessman in the community. I was bragging to him about all the college scholarship offers I was getting and he looked up at me and said, "You'll never go to college because your family is too stupid."

Oh, that hurt. I tried so hard to prove myself to people in the town, but there seemed to always be someone ready to shoot me down with a reference to my brothers and their disabilities. The jabs and put-downs caused me to put even more pressure on myself. I participated in nearly every school activity I could get into. I was a drum major and a class leader and an athlete. And yet, back then it seemed like nothing I accomplished could erase that stigma.

Four years later, after completing college, I was back in Whitesboro and I stopped by T. A. Richardson's place. I was wary of him still, but he surprised me by greeting me warmly and telling me how proud he was that I'd gotten my degree. I didn't remind him of what he had said to me. He had probably forgotten it, but I certainly hadn't. Now I wonder if he said that cruel thing to me in order to motivate me. It was painful, and it is still painful to recall, but his words certainly did motivate me. In times when school wasn't going well, I'd think about what T.A. had said, and then I'd get back to work.

We all have our insecurities that affect our behavior and our view of the world. People tell me that I appear to be a confident guy, but a lot of my drive to be a leader and to push myself to succeed on my own terms is fueled by insecurity and the desire to always prove myself worthy. There will always be those people who look for reasons to put you down in order to elevate themselves. It's a fact of life.

As a child, I didn't really understand that, I felt like I was the only one in the world who had a problem. I felt I was alone in my insecurities, and I felt I had to make it alone. I know now that we all have problems. We all have obstacles to overcome. I have come to understand also that there are many people willing to accept and help you, if only you first accept and help yourself. It's true. If you are an angry person, the hostility drives people away from you, but if you are at peace and have confidence in yourself, people are drawn to you.

## BEING A STAR BASED ON WHO YOU ARE

My sisters tell me that I was fortunate in many ways because sports gave me an outlet to channel my frustrations and a basis for establishing my own identity outside the family. I vented my anger by aggressive play, and I built my identity on my athletic accomplishments. I was a leader in school because I was driven to prove that I was someone of value. In a sense, I did the right thing with my shame and anger. I turned it into positive energy in athletics and in school, rather than acting out violently or anti-socially. But I did the right things for the wrong reasons. Actors talk about using the pain from their personal lives in their work; I did that in my own way, but I didn't let go of the pain. My goal was always to prove myself worthy, rather than to better myself and those around me. I had a chip on my shoulder, and I was always daring the world to knock it off. In the long view, then, athletic ability is not the strongest basis for self-esteem, or at least, it should not be the sole source of someone's concept of self-worth. In most cases, it is simply too shallow a base to support a lifetime of achievement.

Some athletes never come to realize this. It saddens me sometimes when I see young people who believe, as I did, that their talent in sports will be their meal tickets for a lifetime. It disturbs me when I hear kids on the playground saying that they don't need to study or go to school because they are going to make it to the pros and make "the big bucks." I've written in my column for *Inside Sports* that sports can be a cruel mistress. After the last game has been played or after the final race has been run, many athletes find themselves unprepared to make a living. In many ways, you can hardly blame young people for buying into all of the hype. After all, it's sold to promising young athletes incessantly in everything from television advertising to their coaches, parents, and fans. "You could be a star!"

Adults who knowingly mislead young people in this regard aren't much better than the guys selling drugs to kids on the street corner. Both are peddling false dreams. When parents, teachers, coaches, and other adults don't stress the value of education and preparation for the real world, they are depriving young people of their futures. Even many of those who do make it to the highest levels of sports fall on hard times after their careers have ended because they spent too much time basking in the glory and not enough time planning and preparing for life after sports.

My former college roommate, Harvey Catchings, who played in the NBA for eleven seasons in Philadelphia, New Jersey, Milwaukee, and Los Angeles, went through some hard times initially because he hadn't prepared himself for life after basketball. A native of Jackson, Mississippi, Harvey, or "Catch," as I call him, was not as footloose as many players during his career, but he admits that he didn't invest much time thinking about what he was going to do with himself upon his retirement. As a result, his first attempt at business failed. But Harvey learned from his errors and he got down to the business of learning about business. He now has a thriving special events, promotions, and management operation while also pursuing a career in broadcasting.

I can relate to Harvey's experience because, like him, I spent a great deal of my life focused on one thing—becoming a professional basketball player. While in high school, I was recruited by some of the very best colleges and universities in the nation. Harvard, Yale, and USC were among the schools that recruited me, but I did not visit their campuses. I knew I could play basketball at those schools. But I had no confidence in my ability to make it there as a student because I hadn't built up a base academically in high school, where I was an average student. I felt that I could be above average as a student but I hadn't developed my learning skills. My limitations were all self-imposed. Sadly, I had accepted, at least in part, the mentality that said, "Nothing good comes out of Whitesboro." I felt it didn't make any difference what I did. I was living down to those negative expectations.

As it was, I chose a well-regarded smaller school, Hardin-Simmons University in Abilene, Texas, where Harvey and I lived and played together. I obtained my undergraduate degree there and received a good education but I have wondered what might have happened if I had gone to an Ivy League school, whether I would have focused more on preparing myself for the real world instead of hanging on to my dream of a professional basketball career. Harvey got drafted, but I didn't, and I was bitterly disappointed. I figured I could have made it in the NBA because I used to slam over him all the time. (Got you, Catch.)

Being a professional athlete was my vision, but it was a limited vision. I didn't have a backup. I hope young athletes today realize that not everybody can make it to the pros; you need to develop your mind as well as your body. When my professional basketball plans didn't pan out, I didn't know where to go with my life at first. I didn't have confidence in my ability to compete off the basketball court. The old childhood insecurities still weighed me down.

My struggles to find my way in the world illustrate the negative effects of a poor self-image and how low self-esteem can hold you back in life unless you get a handle on what it is that is holding you back and free yourself of it. I have a friend with similar self-esteem problems and it's easier for me to see it in him than in myself. I see him reaching out for validation all the time. He is an overachiever driven to prove himself to the world. I understand him completely, but I often wish that he could learn to accept himself without needing the constant approval of others. That was my problem too, and it is one I still sometimes struggle with.

In many ways, of course, I was very fortunate. My parents were hardworking folks who provided all six of us with all we needed. We lived in a comfortable, four-bedroom home with a huge yard. Because of my athletic skills, I was able to obtain a college education. I have had many opportunities. This is not intended to be an "Oh, poor, pitiful me" story. I simply want to relate to you that in some way all of us experience self-doubt. I have. Nearly everyone I know has had something in his or her background that triggers insecurities. We can all overcome those insecurities to better our lives, and the lives of those in our communities.

At some point in our lives, most of us need help in overcoming whatever it is that is holding us back, whether it is racism, sexism, elitism, or any other obstacle that stands between you and your dreams and aspirations. Oprah forced me to confront my own insecurities but it only sank in after several heated discussions. In particular, I remember a party in Aspen with a lot of celebrities and influential people, all of whom wanted to stand next to Oprah. As the night wore on, I found myself getting pushed further and further away as they moved past me to get to her. Most didn't bother to speak to me, and it really bothered me. I was allowing others to be the keeper of my soul. I know that now. I also realize now that the further you pull away from people, the further they pull away from you, yet if you exude confidence in yourself, people are drawn to you. Oprah tried to make me understand that the real source of my pain was in my past.

"Those old wounds haven't been healed. They are the source of your anger and pain. You are always looking for other people to validate your worth because your family never dealt with your brothers' mental disability or taught you how to deal with it. That's why you are so easily offended," she told me.

I didn't accept her judgment at first. I stewed over her words for a long time before I finally acknowledged that she was right. I realized I was carrying around a great deal of anger and pain. I had the lingering sense that no one respected me unless I demanded it. Because of those insecurities rooted in childhood and adolescence, I had built an emotional shell around those hurtful memories to protect myself. I didn't deal with them, or acknowledge them, but they were still working on me.

## DIGGING DEEP TO HEAL THE PAIN

I can't adequately express how painful it was for me to delve into this area of my psyche after Oprah challenged me to look within. Imagine a toothache that hurts so bad you can't think, and then imagine going in with probes and dental tools trying to dig out the source of the pain and only aggravating it. The journey of self-discovery can be as hurtful, but it can also be enlightening and, ultimately, liberating.

Eventually, I came to understand myself far better than I ever had. I realized that for years my feelings of inadequacy were locked inside, masked by my outwardly confident appearance and manner. Like many people, I can be strong when the challenge is presented; I am at my best when my back is against the wall—in fact I enjoy pressure situations. But there is also a side of me that is not strong, or confident, or always in control. When I'd get hurt, whether from a real or imagined slight, my old insecurities would boil to the surface and eventually erupt.

When I was a younger man, that eruption might trigger a fight, or an argument, but as I learned to control my explosive temper, the anger ate me up inside. I had no protection from what came from within. No protection from my own involuntary reactions. In a sense, I was like people who put steel bars on the windows of their homes and apartments to keep burglars and muggers out. The problem is, if there is a fire inside the dwelling, those steel bars don't protect them, they trap them inside so that there is no escape from the danger within.

Oprah is a big fan of author Marianne Williamson, who writes about this sort of thing often. "Somewhere, sometime . . . we loved with the openness of a child, and someone didn't care, or laughed, or even punished us for the effort," she writes in her book *A Return to Love*. "In a quick moment, perhaps a fraction of a second, we made a decision to protect ourselves from ever feeling that pain again." But, as Williamson notes, when we build barriers "to protect the places where the heart is bruised," we often end up creating the very thing "that we defend against"—more pain.

That is what I did as a young man, to protect myself from those who devalued me and my family because of my brothers' mental disabilities. And because of that protective shell I put up around my inner emotions, I became the victim of my own unvented anger. When incidents such as the one in the drugstore or at the Aspen party occurred, I would fill with rage and hurt.

Your ability to pursue success depends to a large degree on how well you know yourself and the factors that influence your behavior. Most of those who succeed in achieving their goals do it by creating an *environment for opportunity*. They feel that they are *entitled* to go after what they want in life. How do they do that? They open themselves to positive change by becoming positive, energized people. They don't limit themselves with a poor self-image or a negative attitude. They get rid of negative baggage that holds them back. They believe in themselves, giving others cause to believe in them.

## CONFIDENCE, COMPETENCE, AND CAPABILITY

I'm not suggesting that achieving success is easy. It is not. But if you can understand who you are and where you want to go, if you can believe in the possibilities for your life, and if you feel like you deserve your dreams and goals, you are well on your way in the process.

I believe that if you want to create a vision for your life and then follow that vision you must have:

1. Confidence: You must believe in yourself and feel worthy of your vision. You have to feel that you deserve success. You gain

confidence by concentrating on the talents and attributes and personal history that make you special and unique.

2. Competence: You must have the knowledge, training, and skills to find solutions to the problems you encounter and to find the process for success. You develop competence by slowly building upon your skills first in one area and then another through hard work and perseverance.

3. Capability: You must feel capable of defining, creating, and controlling your own life. Again, you can do this by working on your self-discipline, by making a list of personal goals and objectives. Start small with something such as losing five pounds or walking five miles a day. Do it, and then challenge yourself to do something else, such as thirty-minute workouts each day, or reading an inspirational book each week. If you master each of these small goals and objectives, over time you can work up to much bigger ones, proving to yourself and others that you have the power to control your life.

If you grew up with a strong support system that instilled a positive self-image, chances are you have more than adequate reserves of confidence, competence, and capability, or at least you know how to develop them if you commit yourself to doing it. People with positive self-images believe in themselves, in their abilities, and in their power to control their own lives.

There are many causes of negative self-esteem. A child who is constantly criticized and deprived of praise will accept that inferior image of himself or herself. The child will believe that he does not have the power to influence his circumstances. The child's vision becomes severely limited, and his life a self-fulfilling prophecy. He lives down to the low expectations rather than up to high expectations. People who feel that they have little or no value do not feel worthy of success. They do not feel as though they deserve to have their deepest needs and desires recognized or realized.

The messages people listen to and believe as adults are those that were confirmed in them as children. We learn to be who we become. Some learn to be successful and happy adults. Others learn not to expect too much from life. The good news here is that all learned behavior can be changed, even those behaviors that we learned unconsciously in childhood. But first, we have to become aware of where that behavior originates. Self-awareness is a key to self-acceptance, which drives self-motivation and self-fulfillment.

I know now that you have to look within yourself and you have to look to the people and resources available to help you. You have to have someone you trust and believe in help you see and tell you the truth. You have to learn to step back and see yourself and your life with a clear vision. And then, you have to begin to rebuild your base, your foundation, your strength, so that you can face life. You have to learn to *rescript* your life so that instead of following the old self-defeating patterns, you create new paths to follow. If you don't like what you've been getting out of life, you have to change the way you've been approaching it; the bad habits, the negative self-image, all of that has to be redesigned and redefined.

## SELF-EXAMINATION AND SELF-RENEWAL

If you don't examine the inner forces at play within your subconscious, you'll never understand yourself or the world around you accurately. You have to honestly evaluate yourself. We all offer the world what we consider to be our best "face." We all act somewhat differently in the privacy of our homes and with our innermost circle of family and friends. And, finally, we all have a "secret self" that is involved in self-examination of what drives us emotionally and physically.

When you learn to bring that secret self to the forefront, to be honest with yourself and others about your motivations and drives, you begin to see the world more clearly and others see you more clearly too. When you are more comfortable and less guarded with others, you interact with them better. How do you do that? First of all, you examine your inner motivations and feelings, and you come to terms with them by understanding what influences your behavior. Then you create a vision for your life that focuses on your potential and the possibilities rather than on your past and the limitations you've had. You open yourself up to be influenced by others and to influence them in return. In order to recognize our real possibilities and to create a vision for our lives, we first have to get a solid grasp on the feelings and beliefs that have held us back and limited our sense of confidence, competence, and capability.

We can change those feelings and beliefs by identifying the messages that undermine our self-awareness and self-acceptance, and replacing those messages with more positive reinforcements.

Instead of responding, *That guy was being disrespectful of me, he was telling me I'm nothing other than Oprah's boyfriend,* I have learned to change my inner dialogue: *This guy doesn't know me except through Oprah's fame. He is just excited at seeing someone he considers a celebrity, and he said the first thing that came out of his mouth. You can handle it.*

In restructuring our inner dialogues, we restore our sense of confidence, competence, and capability, which allows us to begin building positive experiences while eliminating the negative self-image and sense of helplessness that leave us feeling victimized and inadequate. It takes courage to confront our negative thoughts and to admit that our responses in the past were wrong.

This is not a process that can easily be accomplished alone. Perhaps the most helpful thing for me has been my exposure to positive and dynamic people and the way they live their lives. Some of them are affluent people, celebrities and successful businessmen and women. Others are quietly striving. All have widened my perspective on the world.

Oprah, of course, has played a major role. We have, in truth, served each other in that capacity. I have helped her find her way in times of self-doubt, and she has certainly done the same for me. Each of us has a scarred family history. As someone relentlessly given to self-analysis, she opened herself up much sooner to the childhood traumas that haunted her into adulthood. As an intensely private and introspective person, I took much longer to let the light in, and still, I open the door to it little by little, one ray at a time.

One thing that helped me, and that I recommend to you, is to take time to also examine the positive aspects of your life and take an account of the positive things that add to your sense of self-worth. This can be a positive aspect of your personality, your talents and gifts, or it could be something or someone of value in your personal history or background. I remember picking up a book in my hometown library one day and finding an account of the life of my great-uncle former U.S. Congressman George H. White. It was so inspiring and it gave me a sense of history and value to know that he was part of my family. He was a lawyer who practiced in Washington, D.C., and Philadelphia, and a major landowner and developer along the Jersey shore. In Congress before the turn of the century, he created legislation and lobbied for fairness, equality, and justice.

U.S. Representative White introduced the first anti-lynching legislation on the federal level. In his farewell to his fellow congressmen, who had not welcomed him because he was a black man, he called upon them to "obliterate race hatred, party prejudice, and help us to achieve nobler ends, greater results, and become satisfactory citizens."

There are other high achievers in my family, and as part of my efforts to heal old wounds, I've focused on those people and celebrated their lives rather than dwelling on negative images. Take time now to do your personal accounting of the things that may be holding you back and also the things that can be used to boost you up.

## CHECKING YOUR OWN ID

Describe your five best attributes: What do you like about your-self? Are you hardworking? Kind? Thoughtful? What do other people tell you that they like about you?

1. _____

2. _____

3. _____

4. _____

5. _____

Write down something in your personal history or back-ground that is a source of pride: _____

_____

_____

_____

Now, unload some baggage. Are there any feelings, resent-ments, personal tragedies, or insecurities that may be holding you back in life? Write them down.

_____

_____

_____

_____

_____

Describe below the ways that your own emotional baggage has influenced your behavior in a nonproductive or self-destructive manner.

_____

_____

_____

_____

Make a list of ways in which you can monitor and manage your emotions and eliminate self-destructive or nonproductive behavior. Refer to this list when you feel that some emotional baggage is hindering you or causing you to act in a nonproductive manner.

_____

_____

_____

Finally, write a description of the type of person you want to become: What characteristics do you want to have that you don't have now? What do you admire in others that you don't see in yourself?

_____

_____

_____

_____

_____

Identify someone close to you with whom you can comfortably discuss what you have written in these exercises. Ask for that person's assessment and suggestions. Listen and accept what is said as constructive criticism. As you follow the steps in the Success Process, refer back to these exercises and check your progress in elevating your levels of self-awareness and managing your feelings and emotions in a more productive manner.

Be patient with yourself. Don't expect immediate results, but do open yourself up to growth through increased self-awareness. Know that we are all flawed, but that we also all have gifts to develop and to share. As you accept yourself and learn self-awareness, you will find that it doesn't matter so much how other people treat you or perceive you. You will find that you are far less reactive to their perceptions of you, and more forgiving and accepting of both your flaws and weaknesses and those of people around you. You will begin to be far more dynamic in pursuing a better life for yourself and those you care about.

*Chapter 3*
# Create Your Vision

>>>>>>>>>>>>>>>>

*Who I am is what fulfills me and fulfills the vision I have of the world.*

AUDRE LORDE

I WAS AN All-American kid. Boy Scouts, Sunday school. Church choir. Little League. We had gangs then in Whitesboro, but we didn't know anything about the Crips and the Bloods, or the Gangster Disciples. Our gangs were more like pint-sized versions of our favorite sporting teams. We called our gangs "The Seventy-Sixers" after the Philadelphia 76ers and the "Yanks" after the New York Yankees.

My fellow "gang" members, Marshall Martin, alias "Fuzzy," Richard "Hammerhead" Adams, Curtis and George Davis, Leonard "Hippie" Smith, Carl "Boogie" Matthews, and Alvin "Bootie Doc" Edwards, all shared an interest in sports, which kept us out of trouble except for my one brush with the law. Yes, I now would like to reveal to you *the truth about my criminal past.*

I was a minor league sneak thief. Nearly every Saturday, for a while, my fellow ace burglars and I snuck into Whitesboro Elementary School. Looking back, I don't quite understand where this impulse came from, but I've talked to a lot of other people who did the same thing as kids. Even though you spend half your life trying to get out of school, there seems to be this need to sneak back in when school is closed. It was a cheap thrill, I guess, jimmying the school doors with a penknife like James Bond after some secret government files. One day, we got into my cousin Stevie Blanks's of classroom and I found the schoolboy equivalent of secret files—his teacher's grade book. Stevie was smart so I didn't have to change many of his grades, but I decided to enhance the scholastic achievements of some other friends. Mostly, I changed their Ds to Bs and the Fs to As. They hadn't figured out how to do it in the classroom, so I did it with a few simple strokes of the pen in the gradebook.

My simple pen strokes might have gone unnoticed if I'd simply remembered to put the teacher's pen down when we exited the scene of our crimes that day. But I made two fatal mistakes. Being the master criminal, I'd accidentally dropped and left behind a note with my name on it that my mother had written. Clued in by the note found at the scene of my crimes, a policeman came up to me after school a few days later and questioned me about Whitesboro Elementarygate. During the playground interrogation, he noticed that I had a nice pen in my shirt pocket—the one I had forgotten to put back in the drawer of my cousin's teacher's desk. The policeman asked me where I'd gotten the pen, and I told him I'd bought it at the five-and-dime. He put me in the squad car and said he was going to drive me down there to make sure I was telling the truth.

Most guys probably would have caved in right there. But I was a tougher case, a hardened criminal. I didn't crack. Not then, anyway. It wasn't until he had parked the squad car in front of the five-and-dime that I gave up the goods. Then I sang like a canary. *I confess! I took it from the school! I'll never do it again!*

That was the beginning—and the end—of my life of crime. My parents made it clear to me that they would not tolerate any behavior or activities that might take me down the wrong path. They did it with discipline, but they also served as examples through the way they lived their lives. Though we had our burdens as a family, my parents always stressed to us the virtues of hard work, honesty, and trustworthiness. That was how they lived their lives and how they expected their children to live theirs.

## LIMITED VISION, LIMITED LIVES

As a teenager, I had the distractions that all kids face but I stayed out of trouble because my parents let me know they expected more of me. Gang membership held no allure to me. I had better things to look ahead to. In those years, I had a vision of getting an athletic scholarship to college and going on to professional basketball. That vision kept me on track. I didn't get into any more trouble, except for foul trouble on the court, that is. I played rough in basketball because I felt I had a lot to prove out there. At least I kept the rough stuff within the game. Too many young people take it to the street. They think they have to prove themselves there, but that can be a fatal mistake, and too often it is. I knew of good kids from good families in my town who somewhere took the wrong turn into dead-end lives. We all know of people we grew up with who had promise but threw it away. I know more than a handful of people who fell into lives of crime and drugs. Some went to prison. Some never made it that far.

Those who choose the way of the street do it because they have a limited vision of where their lives can go. They don't look beyond the street to the college campuses and professional buildings and business towers. They don't know what they don't know. They don't have a plan, and because of that they don't have a clue.

Young people don't join gangs because it appeals to them more than a career in medicine or more than the life of an environmental engineer. They join gangs because that is all they see for themselves. Their vision for their lives is severely limited.

They see *Cosby Show* reruns on television, but the idea of being black and a doctor is purely fantasy. They see the gangs, and that is their reality. They join because they have no other source of validation, no greater vision. No plan. No dream. Gang membership gives them an identity that they have not been able to establish elsewhere—in school, at home, in athletics, or in the job market. But this is a form of identification that, in the end, leads nowhere.

Even if it does not lead to gang membership or crime, a lack of a vision for where you want to go in life inhibits your development and growth as a person. You cannot be successful if you have no vision or if you don't feel worthy of success. Having a vision for your life allows you to live out of hope, rather than out of your fears.

## DECIDING WHERE YOU WANT TO GO

After you have taken the first step in the Success Process by working to attain heightened *self-awareness* and to manage your feelings and emotions in a productive manner, the next step is to look at the qualities that you bring to the table and the interests that you have so that you can *develop a vision* of where you want to go in life. This is your life's destination. It is where you want to go in your journey through the Success Process. And so, you must choose it carefully, with a great deal of thought. There is not much worse than going on a long and hard journey only to discover upon arrival that it's the wrong place for you. If you don't feel absolutely certain about the vision you have created for your life, you may not have the enthusiasm and drive and dedication necessary to get there. But if you act wisely at this stage, the rewards will be great upon your arrival.

Think of people you know who appear to be truly happy with their lives, and I'll wager that they are doing exactly what they want to do, living where they are glad to live. Those are people who are living within the vision they chose for their lives. I know that I have never been happier than when I am working on my dreams and visions for a better life. It energizes me because I know exactly where I want to go. This is what Stephen Covey refers to as *beginning with the end in mind.* It is one of his most basic and most useful concepts. If you know where you want to end it, it gives purpose and direction to the journey of your life.

I have seen what happens to people who lack a vision for bettering their lives. When I worked for the federal prison system, I saw hundreds of men who had no such vision beyond their basic instincts to survive. They had no guidelines for their lives, no perception of how to fit within society As a result, they had not been able to work within the system to improve the quality of their lives. Because of their narrow, predatory mind-sets, they had grown up taking what they wanted, and hurting without the least thought to the agony they dealt out. Without consciences, they did not think, they acted. And so they ended up in a place where they didn't have to think, a place where their actions are dictated to them. They are told when to eat, when to sleep, what to wear. In prison, you don't need to know who you are; you need to know only the number on your shirt. That is no way to live. In giving up their responsibilities to society, these men gave up their freedom and became virtual slaves instead.

As head of the education department at the federal prison in Chicago, I saw the records of inmates and their crimes, and, in general, their histories did not vary much. Most broke early in their lives from the framework of society because they were never taught how they fit in, or how the process worked. They never saw their connection to success, and so instead they connected to failure. In search of the easy way out, they instead followed the hardest path, from truancy to delinquency to misdemeanors and felonies. It is a path that leads to nothing but pain.

It's ironic, but mostly sad, that prisons are full of people who, early on, made the decision that no one was going to tell them what to do, and so they ended up in a place where the only option is to do what they are told to do. Every minute of every day of every month and year. Very few of them will ever admit that they are in prison as a result of their own decisions, their own actions. It is always the fault of someone or something outside of their control. Those who do take responsibility for their lives sometimes change their lives by changing their vision of themselves, but too often, for many of them it is too little too late.

If you do not accept responsibility for your own life, your own success, you will never better your life. Those who do not love and respect themselves are incapable of seeing the value of life— for themselves or anyone else. Our prisons are full of men and women whose own self-hatred fueled their contempt for the lives of those whom they have murdered, raped, robbed, or otherwise preyed upon. Not all people with low self-esteem become criminals, of course, but it is rare to find a criminal who does not operate from a perspective of predatory self-hatred and extremely limited vision.

Because of limited vision, they are not aware of all the opportunities that life presents to those who dare to dream and set goals according to their vision for their lives. If you grow up with no frame of reference other than gangs and street life, odds are that is where you will end up, unless you develop a greater vision either on your own, or with the assistance of someone who wants a better life for you.

*Imagine a neighborhood with run-down apartments lined with unkempt lawns and dead bushes. There is no real yard to play in. The only form of activity available to kids is a weathered cement basketball court with a few chain links acting as a hoop. The make-believe walls protect the players from the real world outside . . . the drug dealing and gang activity . . .* That is how NBA All-Star Larry Johnson, a member of

Athletes Against Drugs, describes his childhood world when he gives speeches for AAD.

Larry grew up in South Dallas. It was a tough, stripped-down environment, but fortunately for him, he had a mother devoted to seeing him pursue a better life, he had athletic ability, and he had a vision that kept him off the streets and out of the violent world of gang membership. *Setting goals is the key to staying drug- and alcohol-free,* Larry says. *Whether you want to be a fireman or a politician, once you know what you want out of life you will make sure nothing gets in the way of achieving success. You must focus on what it takes to get you where you want to be.*

## CREATING A VISION FOR A BETTER LIFE

### STEP ONE: TAKE INVENTORY

Creating a vision first requires that you ask yourself what it is that gives meaning and joy to your life, and then find a way to make your life an expression of that joy. Perhaps you like to sing; it gives you joy. Now even if you can't land a record contract, you can still sing as a way of life, whether as a professional performer, as a teacher, or in the church choir, or you could work within the industry to help others develop or market their talents. You may not be able to do exactly what you want to do, but there are a lot of ways to approach your dream.

Your talents are your gifts and when you express those gifts, the world opens up to you. If you develop your talents, people and resources will come to you. And I believe that the true meaning of success is using your talents and abilities—your gifts—to better not only your life, but the lives of those around you.

Many people think that a talent has to be so pronounced that it hits them over the head, and if they haven't been hit over the head with it they say things like, "I don't have any talents." But the truth is, often you express your talents so naturally that you may not recognize them. What you love to do is generally what you naturally do well and what you have been doing all your life, although for most of your life you have probably done it without thinking of being compensated.

Consider the personalities and attributes of people you know in certain professions or fields of work. Nurses are usually naturally nurturing people. Teachers are people who enjoy sharing knowledge. Business managers are well-organized people with leadership qualities. Salesmen are gregarious and enjoy meeting people. Comedians were always the class clowns.

Often people claim that they don't have any identifiable talent, and it may be true that they don't have a gift or special ability that is commonly identified as a talent, such as singing talent, or writing talent, or athletic talent. Everyone, however, has some special ability or keen interest that can be developed, whether it is a knack for doing mechanical things, for building things, or for working well with other people.

It is not difficult to determine what your special ability or gift or interest is. Simply ask yourself. What is it that you enjoy doing most? What gives your life meaning? What do you look forward to doing more than anything else? Ask yourself what is it that you would do with your life even if you didn't get paid for it? Ask yourself those questions and write the answers below.

_____

_____

_____

_____

Although when I was younger I felt my basketball talents would take me into the NBA, that dream didn't work out. After I played several years in the European league, I had to sit down and take inventory of the talents that I could build upon for the rest of my life. I began just as I advised you to begin, by trying to determine what my other talents and interests were.

When I had difficulty getting started, as you might have, I tried a different tactic. I began eliminating the things I *didn't* want to do. I didn't want to be a cog in a machine, I wanted to be the engine, so I knew I wasn't cut out for corporate life unless it was going to be *my* corporation. I had done some modeling, but that was mostly a lark to pick up a little spending money. It wasn't serious enough business for me. I had tried military life and had enough of it.

When I left the army and the European basketball league to return to the U.S., I took a job near Denver with the federal prison system just as a way to pay the bills, and to also be able to do a lot of downhill skiing, which I had learned to really enjoy while overseas. After working for several years with the prison system, however, I decided I didn't want to work in that field all of my life. I was drifting, which may be the position you find yourself in now. Most of my life, I have had a vision of where I was going, and I found it unsettling to be directionless.

And so I instinctively began the inventory process again. After going through a number of possible career ideas that did not appeal to me, my mind was beginning to form a vision of what did interest and excite me. I began looking at the things and activities that I enjoyed being involved in. I realized that I liked to be creative and to work with creative people, and also that I wanted to somehow get back to being involved with the sports and entertainment fields. That was where my talents and interests were. Maybe I could no longer be a player, but I could still be involved. With those things in mind, I was beginning to get a concept of what I wanted to do, but I needed to take that concept the next step.

## STEP TWO: TAP INTO YOUR IMAGINATION

Once you have decided what talents and interests you want to engage in your pursuit of a better life, how do you form a vision around them? You begin by doing what a child does during play: *you use your imagination to create your reality.* A friend of mine told me that his two children, a boy, nine, and a girl, five, play together for hours and hours. Their favorite game is one they made up. They call it their "Imagination Game." Each of them takes a toy figure and they then take turns creating a story in which their figures interact. The only complaint you hear when they play is when one of them tries to dominate the story line, then you'll hear them say, "You're not letting me use my 'magination!"

It is often true that as adults we forget things we understood as children. This boy and girl realize the importance of seeing possibilities with your mind. Often our adult minds are too cluttered, too busy, too overwhelmed to see what children know. Adults can use their imagination to learn about themselves and to explore the possibilities for their lives by allowing themselves to hope and dream about ways their lives could be different.

When I encourage you to dream and to use your imagination, I am not encouraging you to fantasize about finding a pot of gold on your doorstep. Fantasies are frivolous dreams. They can be fun but they are dangerous if we spend so much time fantasizing that we neglect reality. Dr. Martin Luther King Jr. once said, *We must use time creatively, and forever realize that the time is always ripe to do right.* It is best to focus on dreaming within the realm of your experience. It does little good for a college accounting major to fantasize about becoming a multimillionaire overnight. Why? Because in that fantasy the student is awarding himself the goal without envisioning the process. It is far better to use your imagination to see the steps laid out in front of you from college student to graduate to certified public accountant and on through the executive or entrepreneurial ranks.

Grown-ups, particularly athletes and artists, refer to this as the *visualization process*. Great quarterbacks say that they can "see" the proper receiver get open and catch a pass before it is even thrown. Artists talk about visualizing the finished work before they have begun it. To dream is different from fantasizing. To dream is to envision the possibility of something that is not only desirable, but attainable based on who you are, and where you can go in life. By rejecting fantasies but allowing yourself to dream within that context, you can create a new reality, and new possibilities for your life.

When I decided what talents and interests I wanted to apply to bettering my life, I then began to dream of possible applications. Sports broadcasting was one area I explored; other possibilities could have included designing a line of sportswear or sporting equipment, writing a column on sports, coaching, being a sports or fitness trainer, or managing the careers of athletes.

What if your talent and interests lie in writing? You might consider magazine or newspaper journalism, television news writing, playwriting, teaching literature or creative writing, or writing fiction, nonfiction, newsletters, or advertising copy. There are many applications for most interests and talents. I know of a Chicago man whose interests include law, writing, and marketing. He did not go to law school, so he couldn't be a lawyer. He felt he could not support his family by working as a writer. And he was unable to find a job he liked in marketing. But he is now very happy in his job as head of marketing for a law firm.

Make a list of ten different ways you can apply your talents and interests so that you can pursue a better life while doing something that you enjoy doing. Write down everything that comes to mind, even if it seems crazy. Get your imagination working, your creative juices flowing.

1. _____

2. _____

3. _____

4. _____

5. _____

6. _____

7. _____

8. _____

9. _____

10. _____

Many of these things are within the realm of possibility for you, aren't they? Get in the habit of regularly thinking of the possibilities for you and your talents. Open your mind and expand your vision of where those talents can take you and how you can build your life around doing what you love to do.

Now, pick the one thing on that list that most excites you, something you want to do for the rest of your life, something you know you could do for the rest of your life whether you get paid for it or not. (You don't have to completely give up the other ideas on the list; they can be your hobbies or sidelines, just as I have continued to do some of the other things I dreamed up.)

The thing I would enjoy doing for the rest of my life is:

_____

_____

At this point in my own effort to create a vision for my life, I concluded that the best way to put to use my interest in working with creative people and my desire to get back into the sports and entertainment business was to look into a career in public relations and marketing for sports and public events. Sports and entertainment marketing were natural areas for me to explore because of my many contacts in both areas and because I could use those contacts to get my own business started. To truly add to the quality of your life, your vision has to be built around the things that you enjoy doing, that you have a passion for.

## STEP THREE: SET GOALS

Once you have decided what you want to do to create a better life for yourself by developing a vision, the next step is to set goals that will serve as stepping-stones toward fulfillment of your vision. Your goals are extensions of your vision for your life and reflections of your talents and interests and values.

It does no good to simply set goals unless you devote some thought to creating truly meaningful goals. A car thief has goals. So does Mother Teresa. The difference is in the quality of their vision and their focus. Go over the following questions when considering how your vision is going to be focused.

What do you want to accomplish in your life?

_____

_____

_____

What do you want to leave behind as your legacy?

_____

_____

_____

What foundation will your goals be built upon? What values, beliefs, or principles matter most to you?

_____

_____

_____

Why do you want to achieve your goals? Will society benefit? Will those around you? Is it linked to things you believe in?

_____

_____

_____

To be effective, your goals must focus also on where you want to be each step of your journey so that as you proceed, you can always determine how far you've come and how much further you have to go. Your goals move you along and they also confirm your mission as you go. They add to the meaning of what you are doing and they give you and those around you a strong sense that you are in control of your life.

There are eight guidelines for goal-setting to keep in mind:

## 1. *Goals must be realistic.*

Just as your vision for a better life should be well-grounded in reality rather than fantasy, your goals must be attainable as well as designed to build gradually, so that the more difficult goals are set nearer to the end of the journey when you have built up confidence and determination. If your vision of a better life includes starting your own business, for example, you don't set early goals for leasing office space in Trump Tower.

## 2. Goals must be meaningful.

Too often, people are limited in their goal-setting. They set shallow or short-term goals for themselves without developing serious long-term goals. The goals you set have to be focused on your vision. You don't set goals that lead you nowhere in particular. Everyone sets goals, and most fall short of them because they don't set goals that have real meaning for their lives. Every New Year's Eve people set goals to get more exercise and get in shape. And by the middle of March the $200 piece of exercise equipment they bought is serving as an expensive clothing rack, unless the goal to get in shape is tied to a greater vision for their lives.

## 3. Goals must be well-defined.

When you set out on a trip you don't generally say, "Sometime soon, I think I'll go a couple hundred miles to the northeast somewhere and get there when I get there." No, you set a specific destination and a specific time when you want to be there. When you set goals in your journey to a better life, you want them also to be well-defined. "I want to make a lot of money" may well be part of your vision, but it is not a well-defined goal. Neither is "I am going to work for the benefit of mankind." A well-defined goal might be "Within the next six months, I am going to raise $10,000 to purchase a home-based business franchise that will help get me started toward my vision of a better life" or "This week, I am going to volunteer to be involved in Junior Achievement at my office in order to help young people understand the business world."

## 4. Goals must excite YOU.

I put the emphasis on *you* because this is your vision for your life. People around you may have good intentions and you should certainly listen and consider all advice they offer, but don't let them throw you off the path of your journey by allowing them to set goals for you that are more in line with their vision than yours.

## 5. Goals should follow a natural progression to a target locked in your mind.

This is the old don't-put-the-cart-before-the-horse warning. Your goals should be step by step so they make perfect sense and so that you always know, out of pure logic, that the next one is within reach and that it moves you toward your destination. If one follows the other, they will remain locked in your mind.

## 6. Goals may need fine-tuning.

Realistically, things can happen as you pursue your vision of a better life, so your goals may require fine-tuning along the way. You may accomplish some easier than you had thought; others may elude you. Keep your vision in mind and make adjustments as you go in order to stay on target. When I was in college, I always figured that when my athletic career ended, I would try to get into a corporate environment where I could spend my entire career. I had that goal in mind, but I didn't know how the process worked. I wasn't a business major and I didn't really have any mentors, and so I was still searching when I got out of college. As time went on, that goal changed because I came up with a bigger dream, of having my own business. The important thing is to keep goals ahead of you at all times. I advise you to do that, but I also want to make it clear that goals are not the ultimate reward. The reward is in pursuing the dream.

## 7. Goals should require positive action.

A primary purpose for setting goals is to get you moving in the right direction. There is really no reason to set goals that don't challenge you to take action. "I am going to consider losing some weight" is not a goal. "At 10 A.M. tomorrow I am going to jog three miles" is a goal. Setting goals within each of your Success Circles, acting upon them, and achieving them not only moves you forward, it builds your confidence in your ability to pursue your vision of a better life. Goals help you act on your dreams rather than just wishing or hoping for them.

## 8. Goals do not isolate you.

Sometimes when people set goals, and even when they establish a vision for their lives, they focus so much on where they want to go, they don't consider what they want to become. You have heard the saying: *Be careful what you go after, it may get you!*

I know of a very smart person whose goal was to become a surgeon. He set his mind on that goal in high school and went after it. The problem was that he was so obsessed with his goal that he neglected most of the rest of his life. He never formed close relationships because they might have distracted him from dedication to his studies. He rarely went to family functions because he didn't want to fall behind in school. He reached his goal of becoming a surgeon, but he has no life outside of his work, and so his life is one-dimensional. He is a lonely guy because he took care of business but he didn't take care of the rest of his life.

I tell my daughter, who is now an economics major in college, that I think it is important for women who become successful in business to learn the lesson of many men who neglect their personal lives in order to focus on their careers. I've advised Wendy to be careful that she doesn't get to her thirties and forties and realize she has focused too much on her career. Your relationships and your personal life are not secondary considerations. There is not a more lonely feeling than walking into a great big house and realizing that beautiful as it is, there is no one home but you.

## Goals Get You Where You Want to Go

So many books and self-help tapes talk about goals without really showing how they can work for you. After a while, you might be tempted to think that goals are just some academic exercise without any real applicability to your life. If that is the case, come into my office here in Chicago, and I'll introduce you to a young man who will testify to the value of setting goals.

A few years ago, I received a letter from a Marquette University student named Chris Janson, from Chicago. He was a marketing major and intensely interested in a career in sports marketing. He had seen my column on that subject in *Inside Sports* magazine and he was inquiring to see if my company had any internships or job openings.

Obviously, Chris had a vision for his life and he had set a goal within that vision, of landing an entry-level job within his field of interest. I wrote Chris back and told him that I didn't have a position for him at that time, but that I'd be happy to talk to him anytime he wanted to come in. Sports marketing is a relatively new field and there weren't a lot of openings at the time, so shortly after I wrote back to Chris, I received another letter from him.

I get a lot of requests for employment, but none quite like this one. Chris responded by offering to work for me *for free* just to get some experience in the field and to make some contacts. Now here is a young man determined to go after his vision, I thought.

Needless to say, I gave Chris a call, invited him to come by, and put him on my staff as an intern. He did work for me in that position for a brief time for no pay, but only until I saw what potential he had, then I put him on a salary. He has worked for me for nearly three years now, and I have no doubt that someday he will have his own sports marketing firm.

Chris knows what he wants to do with his life and he set a goal focused on that, rather than on the immediate financial rewards. He realizes that there are some advantages to starting out in a smaller firm such as mine rather than one of the huge sports marketing companies. At my firm, Chris will get the experience to do it all: marketing, event planning, logistical coordination, every aspect of the business. He has already done things that most account executives in larger marketing firms never are exposed to. And he has made some wonderful networking contacts.

Chris set a goal, acted on it, and changed his life. He should feel very good about that, and it should give him the confidence to set progressively bigger and more challenging goals for the rest of his life. When you identify goals consistent with your vision for a better life, you set a direction just as you would in choosing a destination to sail to on a boat. As any sailor knows, "If you do not know which harbor you are headed for, no wind is the right one." You set goals by understanding what you want to do and where you want to go.

You may come from a disadvantaged background. You may have low self-esteem. But you are free to dream of a better life and then to act upon that dream. There will be challenges in life; we all have our challenges. If you are going nowhere, there is no reason to take on those challenges, but if you have goals and a vision of where you want to go, then you will be motivated to overcome the challenges you encounter. You may not overcome every challenge but if you learn from each of them and hold on to your vision with perseverance, dedication, and hard work, it is almost impossible to be defeated.

Here are some goals I set for myself when I decided I wanted to get into the sports and events marketing business:

- To read and learn as much about this business as possible.
- To find role models whose businesses I could study either up close or from afar.
- To find one or more mentors willing to give me advice and encouragement.
- To make strategic alliances with other individuals, businesses, consultants, and corporations in order to provide a broad range of services.
- To develop a client base across a wide range of sports and types of events.
- To write a mission statement.
- To build a strong network of business contacts tied together through personal relationships.

Now it is your turn. Make a list of ten goals that will help you pursue your vision for a better life.

1. _____

2. _____

3. _____

4. _____

5. _____

6. _____

7. _____

8. _____

9. _____

10. _____

## STEP FOUR: FIND GUIDES AS YOU GO

When I go on a trip to a city or country that I have not visited before, I make it a point either to find someone I know who has been there and ask them for tips on places to go and things to see, or, when I arrive, to talk to people who live there and seek their advice. I think this is good policy for traveling. It has helped me discover places and things I might have walked right past if I hadn't taken the time to ask for advice. And it has also helped me avoid some bad spots and potential dangers.

I believe that good things happen to those who look for them. When you open yourself to life, then life comes to you. I have friends who believe that we all put out our own unique form of energy, sort of a wavelength. And they believe that people who are on the same wavelength respond to your energy. If we put out angry energy, we attract people with anger in them, but if we put out positive energy, positive people are drawn to us, and our combined energy leads to more positive things. You have to admit, this theory makes some sense. One way to do that is to establish relationships with people who can be your guides in your journey to a better life. Not only can they help you establish goals and pursue them, but they can offer you advice and encouragement along the way.

One of my guides, or mentors, is Bob Brown of High Point, North Carolina, who is widely known as a source of wisdom and guidance for African Americans seeking to make it in the business world. I met Bob at a social gathering back when I was just trying to get started in business. We started talking and I immediately liked him. I just gravitated toward him. It happens in life. If you are looking to better yourself, you will draw people like him to you.

I thought he was a very distinguished guy—"statesmanlike" is the word that came to mind, even before I discovered he had once served as a special assistant in the White House. He is very well connected, and he has an air of confidence and accomplishment. A perceptive person, as might be expected of someone who has been in the public relations business nearly three decades, Bob sensed that I wanted to better my life.

He owns B&C Associates, an international public relations firm serving Fortune 500 clients and many very influential figures, particularly people in state and local government. When we first met, Bob made public relations and marketing sound fascinating. It is a field of relationships and contacts. It is a business that demands a high level of creativity and communication and people skills. And it is also a field with a lot of wonderful opportunities. Bob introduced me to one of those opportunities when he invited me to accompany him on a trip to the Ivory Coast in Africa, where he was working with the government to attract business investors.

He offered the additional lure of being his golf partner on the trip. Although I am now an avid golfer, I had played only a few times before that and I didn't even own a set of clubs at that point. But I didn't want to miss the opportunity to see Bob in action. The experience was incredible. It opened my eyes to many things, particularly to the complexities of international business. It also exposed me to some top-level business minds since all eight of the other people on the trip were serious business executives involved in everything from medical records to newspapers to clothing textiles, food services, and the travel industry.

On the trip, Bob and I forged a friendship and he invited me to join his business, so I moved to North Carolina to work with him. I'd come back to Chicago on weekends to visit but I thought it was important to soak up as much as I could from Bob and his business. My title was vice president of business development, but I was really a trainee. I was green and didn't know really what was going on, so I learned by traveling with Bob. Not that I learned it all, but I did establish a foundation of knowledge in the business.

Bob is still a mentor and role model for me and for a lot of other people. He is the sort of person you attract when you have a vision for your life. Another of his protégés is my friend Armstrong Williams. Armstrong comes from little Marion, South Carolina, and he is like a mini-tornado. He goes after what he wants in life and he is smart, intuitive, and hard-driving. He has that *underdog* mentality that I admire. Today, Armstrong is a very successful author and radio and newspaper commentator in Washington, D.C. Armstrong and I both benefited a great deal from having Bob Brown as a mentor.

Think now of people who have come into your life because they could see what you saw for yourself. These people might be relatives or friends of the family, teachers, coaches, anybody who has stepped in and helped you refine your vision for your life.

Make a list of the people who have stepped up to help you, and next to each name write what they have done.

| Role models and mentors | How you were helped |
| --- | --- |
| | |
| | |
| | |
| | |
| | |

If you can't think of anyone, your problem may be that you have not clearly defined your vision for your life. Remember, you can't expect others to see it for you, if you can't see it for yourself.

Now, make a list of five potential mentors who can help you set goals for the journey to a better life. Make definite and specific plans for contacting these potential mentors and for seeking their guidance.

1. _____

2. _____

3. _____

4. _____

5. _____

## STEP FIVE: PUT ON YOUR BLINDERS

I have long struggled with a problem of staying focused on my goals. It reminds me of the problems I have in my golf swing. I don't follow through, which causes me to lose power and direction when I hit the ball. The same thing occurs when you don't follow through and stay focused in life. You lose power and direction. When you set goals, you have to keep them always in mind. It's not that you can't enjoy other aspects of your life, but those goals always have to be at the forefront. Look at the people in your life, or people that you have read about, who are successful. I'll bet that they are well-focused people who are not easily distracted from their goals, whatever they are. And I bet that no matter what they are doing at any given point in time, it is compatible with their long-term goals.

Recently, a friend of mine offered me free office space. It was a nice gesture of friendship, but my friend didn't understand. In order to stay focused on my goal, I can't afford to accept such generosity. I need to do it for myself. I need to pay my own way. I need to prove to myself that I can do it on my own. To accept free office space would hinder me, it would take away from my need to validate my own identity.

You will have distractions too. You will have temptations. You will occasionally want to coast or take shortcuts even if they take you in the wrong direction. Keep that vision of a better life in your head. It does an Olympic runner no good to shave miles off his training run. True, it may be easier, but it is a waste of time if it doesn't build strength and endurance for him to pursue his ultimate goal.

## STEP SIX: ENJOY THE JOURNEY

I am working hard at building a career and a business for myself, and I am having more fun doing it than anything else I've ever experienced. It is fun to pursue your dreams, and to keep pushing yourself to expand your vision. That's one of the things I share with those closest to me, the drive to keep pushing ourselves but to enjoy it as we go. I could have settled for a career in corrections. I could have settled for any number of comfortable positions with a lot of perks, but the easy route was not the route I had envisioned for myself because it did not take me to the end that I had in mind—I want to achieve success on my own, through my own hard work.

As you progress through your goals, if it begins to seem like a burden, if you find yourself anxious and snapping at people, it may be a warning that you've wandered off track, or perhaps that your vision needs adjustment. At the end of each day, you should be able to see progress, and you should go to bed with a smile on your face because you are proud of what you have accomplished and eager to tackle what remains to be done. Remember, this is a long journey, a life's journey, and you want to be able to savor and enjoy each step along the way.

I enjoy what I am doing to better my life because I see owning a business as the road to true freedom. It represents economic independence and equality. Everyone respects someone who controls his or her own destiny, but most important is the self-respect that comes with creating, striving, and thriving in the marketplace where so many great people have found success.

I take satisfaction also in the challenge of building a successful company that will allow me to leave a legacy for my daughter, my family, and for other people along the way. You know, many people study and work and learn how to run a business or excel in a position only to one day stop and wonder *why* they have taken the path they are on. When you are doing what you love, you may wonder *how* you are going to do it, but you will never wonder *why*.

That's another reason why your vision should not be focused on making money or acquiring things. High living isn't the goal. Elevating others through your life is. Part of my vision is to make a contribution and to give something back to the community, to people of all races, creeds, and colors. I think there is no better way to do that than with a business that creates jobs, opportunities, and financial wisdom for others. The focus of your vision should be on developing and using your talents for the enjoyment and welfare of others as well as for the benefit of you and your loved ones. If you make a lot of money by allowing your talents to flourish, that's great, but making a lot of money shouldn't be your goal. If making money becomes your only focus, your vision will be too narrow. If that is your entire focus, the more money you make, the narrower your focus will become. Soon, your entire life will center around making more money and holding on to that which you have already made.

Far too many people go to their graves with money in the bank but nothing in their hearts. Others lead far more fulfilling lives by elevating the lives of those around them through the expression of their talents and the things they love the most. School-teachers certainly do not make enough money in relation to the importance of their roles in society, particularly at a time when they have to not only teach, but instill values in so many children who do not get what they need at home. Nurses and social workers, policemen and firemen, and the people who make our cities work—all of these people contribute greatly to the quality of our lives without taking home huge paychecks.

Many of these people will tell you that they are doing what is most important to them; they are filling a great need. You have to respect that sort of character. These are people who have created their lives based on something far more rewarding than material goods. They do what they do because it allows them to feel good about themselves. When you are creating a vision for a better life, that is important to keep in mind. What can you do that will allow you to feel good about yourself?

A better life does not necessarily mean more money or a bigger house, or vacations in Europe. A better life can simply mean a life with meaning. A rewarding life. A life that contributes to the common good. A life that nurtures goodness in others. We should all devote ourselves to always searching for ways to live a better life and ways to find truly meaningful success.

## Chapter 4
# Develop Your Travel Plan
>>>>>>>>>>>>>>>

*Before taking steps, the wise man knows the object and end of his journey.*

W. E. B. Du Bois

WHEN MICHAEL JORDAN soars through the air to dunk the basket-ball, is it magic? When Gloria Estefan brings a crowd to its feet with a performance, is that magic? When Maya Angelou recites her poem at the inauguration of a President of the United States and captivates an entire nation with her words, is that magic?

In a way, yes, it *is* magic. It is the magic that is created when people make the most of the talents and abilities and intelligence given them. That magic lies within all of us, even those of us who may not have the extraordinary gifts of a Michael Jordan, Gloria Estefan, or Maya Angelou.

When you watch or listen to those famous people, they seem larger than life, graced and untouched by the day-to-day trials and tribulations that you and I face. Then again, think about this:

- Michael Jordan was cut from his junior high school basket-ball team and had to become the team manager in order to keep practicing with the rest of the players.

- Gloria Estefan had her back broken in a traffic accident at the height of her career, and underwent intensive physical therapy to return to the stage.
- Maya Angelou was raped at the age of eight and, as a result of the mental trauma, she was unable to speak for several years.

In truth, everyone faces hardship and rejection and loss in their lives, even those who may appear to be blessed. There is another truth here: we are *all* blessed in some way. In a very real sense, all of us have a certain *magic*, a gift, a talent, or an ability that if developed and put to its highest use can help us overcome setbacks, defeats, and difficulties. That is the magic within you.

Not all of us can be an All-Star basketball player, or a Grammy-winning recording artist, or a great poet and writer, but each of us has talent and ability that can be channeled into something that will make our lives fulfilling and worthwhile. And that same magic enables us to use our talents and abilities to make the world a better place.

By tapping into your gift and truly believing in your ability to make things happen in your life, you can create your own magic in this world. Now, some people watch Michael Jordan make one of his incredible moves to the basket, or they hear the words of Maya Angelou, and they may be tempted to say that they make it look so easy. But Michael once said, "If there was a most likely to succeed, I was the least." The truth is that people who succeed sometimes make it look easy because they have worked so hard to develop their skills to extraordinary levels. Yes, it takes work to change your life for the better. It takes drive and determination. But by focusing on the magic within, it is possible to go from benchwarmer to star, from a hospital bed to the world stage, and from trauma and muteness to great eloquence.

There is a story often told about an art lover who watched the great artist Picasso create a painting in a matter of only a few hours. The observer naively told the painter that it must be wonderful to be able to create a masterpiece so easily. Picasso is said to have replied indignantly: "You weren't here to watch the forty years of work that went into my art."

I can tell you that my success as a basketball player, modest as it was, came only after I was willing to work long hours developing my playing skills and my physical strength. My successes in business have demanded even more mental preparation, planning, and hard work.

To develop your skills and talents to their greatest potential, you too will have to work hard, overcome difficulties and doubts, and push yourself beyond any levels you may have achieved in the past. But you can do it. It is possible to make a better life for yourself if you develop a plan for going after what you want for yourself.

So far in the previous chapters, I have helped you:

- Increase your self-awareness so that you are in control of emotions and feelings that may have held you back in the past.
- Create a vision of your dreams and goals.

In this chapter, I will help you learn *how to formulate a plan of action* to fulfill that vision by selecting the steps that will move you most efficiently toward your goals within each area of your life, as symbolized by your Success Circles for your relationships, job or career, and your role in the community.

## CHOOSING ACTION STEPS TOWARD YOUR GOALS

Before we start, I'd like to issue a traveler's advisory. Don't go too fast for conditions when planning for your future. I have read that it takes at least five years just to decide exactly what kind of business you want to operate, ten years more of being involved in it before you can legitimately say you are in the business, fifteen years to build it up sufficiently, and twenty years before you can call yourself a real businessman. That applies to other aspects of your life and work too. As Picasso noted, the ability to make things look easy is based in years of hard work.

There really are no shortcuts to lifelong success. Some people become overnight successes, but often they fade as fast as they came on the scene. How many singers or bands are known as "one hit wonders"? How many athletes succeed in professional sports without first spending years developing their skills? Often, the reason people fail after one hit or a brief period of success is that they weren't prepared for long-term success. They didn't build a foundation of knowledge and training and experience.

Whatever your goals, don't rush at them. Effective planning involves identifying those actions that will move you toward your goals as quickly and as efficiently as possible. Once you spend time it is gone, so you don't want to waste your time on steps that don't contribute to your progress toward your goals. My new CD-ROM computer sat on my desk at home for several months before I could take the time to really learn all its capabilities. It is an incredible tool, but for a while I had to focus on critical planning that doesn't require a computer. It was a judgment call on my part. Sometimes you have to remain focused on the first difficult steps before you can begin the rapid climb.

Each of us has limited time, energy, and resources, so it is not possible to do everything that might move us toward our goals. Deciding which steps to take can be difficult, but if you weigh your choices carefully, you can take great strides with a few efficient steps rather than running all over the place trying to do too much. Effective planning involves prioritizing those steps that move you most efficiently toward your goal.

For many of you, simply buying or borrowing this book was one small action taken toward fulfilling a vision for a better life.

See, you probably weren't even aware that you *had* a plan, were you? The fact that you have begun to take action may have already brought about subtle changes in the way you live your life. When you set goals and achieve them by following a plan, you create a certain *magic* by building confidence in your own value and worthiness. You begin to live out of your imagination, looking forward to the possibilities for your life, rather than backward at the limitations and liabilities of your past.

When you begin to actually work toward your goals through a plan of action, you assert power over your life. You prove that you have control. When you live life with purpose and energy by acting upon goals that are based in principles that you believe in, then you are living on your full power. You are fully engaged in life. You know who you are and where you are going and what sort of person you want to be when you get there.

If you set goals and don't go after them, or go after them with a weak plan, you encounter only frustration and disappointment. You feel lost, and others pick up on it. There is nothing magical in someone who has no direction for his or her life. You don't want to rush up and say, *Let me join you in your confusion.* Most of us are drawn to people who have a plan for pursuing their vision for their lives.

How do you develop a plan? Step by step. One foot in front of the other. Following the route that best serves your purposes, whether it is along a well-traveled highway over the river and through the woods, or along untraveled terrain. Selecting the route that is right for you is critical. You don't rush the planning stage of your life's journey any more than you would take off on a long trip without studying the map first to determine the best route for your purposes.

Note that I wrote *for your purposes*. You and I may both be driving to Atlanta from Chicago, but you may have relatives in Chattanooga who would be hurt if you didn't stop by. I may have an old army buddy in Nashville that I'd like to visit. It might be easier if we could all follow the same plan for pursuing our goals, but the fact is, each of us is unique. We each have our own talents, strengths, weaknesses, goals, and vision for our lives. That is why it is so important to take your time to consider all of your options and to select those that are best for you.

I believe in spending a great deal of time planning because it can save you so much time later. If you plan carefully, you avoid wasted time spent dealing with crises and steps that don't move you directly toward your goal.

As a simple example, let's say your goal is to become division manager of Buster's Widget Company, where you are currently a lowly mail room clerk. What are some steps you could take toward your goal?

1. Apply for a management trainee program at Buster's Widget Company.
2. Take night courses in management training at a local community college.
3. Work so efficiently and show such enthusiasm in your mail clerk job that you attract the attention of the current division manager, then let him know you are interested in working directly for him.
4. Ask a longtime employee whom you admire to teach you everything there is to know about the widget business.
5. Subscribe to every widget manufacturing magazine, management training magazine, and motivational magazine you can afford.
6. Sign up to do volunteer work for Buster's favorite charity and impress him with your talents and enthusiasm there in hopes of being moved up the ladder at work.
7. Submit an essay to the National Widget Makers' Association journal detailing your ingenious ideas for making widgets more profitably and efficiently.

8. Join the health club where Buster and all of the top executives of his company work out. Get to know them on that basis and try to impress them with your devotion to the job, knowledge, and enthusiasm.

Obviously some of the tactics listed above would be far more beneficial and valid than others. Some are just plain silly, but at least they are actions that move you *toward* a goal. Pause a minute here and write down twenty things you can do that would move you closer to your goals for your personal life, your career, or your involvement in the community.

If you need help ask a friend, a teacher, counselor, a role model or mentor, or one of your family members to help you brainstorm about actions you might take to move you toward your goals.

1. _____

2. _____

3. _____

4. _____

5. _____

6. _____

7. _____

8. _____

9. _____

10. _____

11. _____

12. _____

13. _____

14. _____

15. _____

16. _____

17. _____

18. _____

19. _____

20. _____

Now, identify four of these twenty items that are likely to have the greatest influence on moving you toward your goal.

1. _____

2. _____

3. _____

4. _____

Did you find it difficult to come up with twenty things? Was it even harder to select the four that would have the greatest impact? Doesn't it feel good, though, to look at those lists and realize that there are so many steps available to you, so many things you can do to move closer to your goal?

Think about your plan for reaching your goal and search for someone who had a similar goal. Study how that person did it. What initial steps did that person take? What worked and what didn't work? Don't be afraid to go to that person and ask questions. You will probably be surprised to find that successful people are willing to share their success with others.

A tried-and-true method for accelerating your learning process is to seek out someone who has already traveled the road you have selected for your journey to a better life. Because I decided to start my own business relatively late in life, I looked for a role model. I would have loved to have enrolled in the Harvard Business School or some other prestigious program in order to receive the best possible business education. That would have made sense for most people. My particular problem was that I really didn't feel I could afford to take two years out of my life to return to school for yet another degree. It would have cost a lot of money, and I was not getting any younger. So, I ruled out going back to school. At this point in my life that didn't seem to be an efficient use of my time, even though it certainly would have been helpful.

Please note that I am in no way suggesting that this is the route everyone should take. If you can get into a quality business school, do it. There is no substitute for a college education, not to mention the value of the contacts you make and relationships you form. It just wasn't the best route for me to take at that stage in my life.

Instead of going to Harvard, I selected someone who'd gone to Yale, and I went to school on his experiences. Interestingly enough, the role model I selected was Cleveland lawyer Mark H. McCormack, founder of International Management Group, a pioneering sports management and marketing company. McCormack was an interesting choice because he is also the author of the best-selling book *What They Don't Teach You at Harvard Business School,* a streetwise guide to business.

Back in the early 1960s, McCormack was just a young lawyer looking for a way to combine his business with his love of golf. He created his vision around something he enjoyed doing, just as I advised you to do in the previous chapter. With an initial investment of only $500 and a wealth of common sense and street smarts, he built a billion-dollar international business, which represents more than six hundred athletes around the world. IMG not only manages the careers of athletes, it also conducts sporting and special events, produces television programming, does marketing for Fortune 500 firms, offers financial planning for top corporate executives, and consults for the Olympics.

I have studied the operations of IMG and implemented many of McCormack's methods and tactics as described in his book. I probably have learned more specific and truly helpful information from him and his company than I might have learned at Harvard because my company plan is so similar to his. A formal education provides you with a great foundation to build upon, but it is hard to beat real-world experience. If you find someone who is doing what you think you may want to do with your life, you might even consider going to work for this role model in order to speed up your own progress. I considered working for IMG, but in the end decided to strike out on my own instead.

In a sense, I was following McCormack's lead there too. Early in his business career, a representative from a huge television production company tried to hire McCormack to run its new sports division. He thought about it, but declined because he wanted to be in business for himself. Instead, he turned around and hired the representative who had been sent to hire him. That representative helped McCormack's own television division become the world's leading independent producer of sports programming.

## GETTING ON SCHEDULE

Determining what crucial actions to take to best pursue your goals is only the first step in enacting your plan. The second step is setting up a well-defined and disciplined schedule to take those actions. Scheduling, according to time management experts, is the *bridge* between knowing what to do and doing it.

When you schedule yourself to do something by picking an exact time to do it, it motivates you to get the task done. Your dentist doesn't say, "Come in any old time and we'll do that root canal." Your car mechanic doesn't say, "Oh just drop it off and I'll get to it one of these days." When you really want something done, you pick a definite time and you get it done.

Normally, I get up at 5:30 each morning and write out my plan for the entire day in my daily journal. I don't do it every day, but I often run into problems when I don't. By writing down my schedule for the day I can find ways to improve the quality and level of what I accomplish. Often, I'll think of someone else I need to see or talk with, or a more efficient way to reach an objective. I also plan for each week and month in advance, and when you stay on top of your schedule in this manner, you stay in control of your life.

What is wonderful about this is that it serves as a constant reminder so you aren't racking your brain for what you should be doing next, plus it serves as a record that you can refer to later.

By scheduling important activities in advance, you don't give up any power over your time. You decide the appropriate time and place. This results in a much more positive and predictable flow for your days, weeks, and months than if you randomly did things whenever you felt like it, or whenever the time seemed right. And so, scheduling ensures you will be more effective in pursuing your goals. It also ensures that you will have the time to do the most important things rather than allowing them to be crowded out or overrun by trivial pursuits.

## GAINING STRENGTH BY THE WEEK

When you create a schedule for your life, the intention is not to dictate what you are going to do every minute of every day. You have to have flexibility to live your life. You have to be able to respond to unexpected events that could be important, and to enjoy yourself too. But you also want to make sure that you get the really important things done. For example, if part of your vision for your life includes foreign travel, somewhere along the line you are going to have to get a passport. If you don't schedule the time to do that, you will likely face a crisis when the opportunity arises to go somewhere outside the country. And too many crises in your life results in chaos, and a life without direction or meaning.

Most time management experts agree that the best scheduling tool is a *weekly calendar*. Doing it weekly rather than daily takes some of the pressure off and gives you a better perspective. Doing it monthly or annually doesn't give you enough flexibility to adapt as you go. Weekly scheduling provides you with a more comfortable pace that won't have you scurrying or burning out. Fitness trainers say the best training cycle for most people is to work out three times a week for thirty minutes and allow your body time in between to rest and build strength. Scheduling your activities on a weekly basis helps achieve greater balance in life, enabling you to achieve success in your personal life, at work, and in your community.

When you set weekly activities to move you toward your goals there are a few things to keep in mind. Remember, first of all, that these short-term goals, like your vision for your life, have to be compatible with your principles, beliefs, and values. You can't be doing things daily or weekly that don't match up with the way you want to lead your entire life and expect to get where you want to go. If your vision for your life is to have children who love you and appreciate you, then you can't spend your days and weeks away from home and not involved in their daily lives. It just doesn't work that way.

Remember the old song "Cat's Cradle," in which the father keeps telling his son that he doesn't have time for him, and then, later in life, the grown son responds to the father's requests with the same answer? You get out of life what you put into it. And the same holds true with relationships.

## NEEDING NO WALLS

When putting together your weekly activity list, resist the typical inclination to think of personal, work, and family activities as separate. They aren't. Things that happen in each aspect of your life affect all other aspects. If my daughter is having problems, it affects me and, often, it affects my ability to concentrate at work. And if things are hectic at work, it affects my personal life and my ability to spend time with my daughter or Oprah. Fortunately, it works the other way too. When things are going well with relationships, it provides stability that makes you more effective in your work.

It is impossible to put one of those shelf organizers in your life and give everything its own neat compartment. It just doesn't work that way. One thing spills over into another. When you are growing in your work, that tends to spur growth in your personal life, and vice versa. And so, if you want to schedule an activity that moves you closer to your goals for your work or career, there is no reason that activity can't also contribute to your goals for your personal or family life. Certainly this applies in physical activity, which can benefit all aspects of your life. But even if the activity is just going to the library to do some research, it is still possible to take along a family member who might enjoy the trip and take the opportunity to share something with you.

It might be wise, however, to set aside certain periods of time for activities that affect specific aspects of your life. Most people with children have sporting events, special lessons, or school activities to attend. And most families make it a point to do things together at some point over the weekend. In your work, it might be wise to set aside time to study the latest information, research, and theories in your field. If you are involved in community work, you'll need to block out time too for meetings and other activities.

Your weekly activities don't have to just be things that you "do." They can be things that you learn, or seek to understand, or share. If you are working on a goal to get an advanced degree, one of your week's activities might be to talk to someone who has gone through graduate school and can tell you what it was like.

Write down the goals you listed earlier, the steps you selected in the previous chapter, and two actions you could take next week that would move you a significant distance toward that goal.

My goal is: _____

_____

The steps I could take to move me toward those goals are: _____

_____

Two activities I could undertake to take those steps are:

1. _____

2. _____

Now, schedule those actions for a specific time on a specific day next week.

I will complete these activities at the following times:

Activity 1: Date _____ Day of Week _____ Time _____

Activity 2: Date _____ Day of Week _____ Time _____

## MUSTERING A WEEK'S WORTH OF WILLPOWER

Looking at the week as a whole allows you to see just how you are spending your time, which helps you make informed decisions about changes you might want to make if you feel you are not moving along swiftly enough toward your goals. Scheduling is a commitment you make to yourself. And looking at your schedule can reinforce your sense that you are in control of your life. It is also important to evaluate how each week went in order to learn from your experiences and to help yourself see what is working for you and what isn't.

You might want to do each evaluation on the back of your weekly schedules or in a separate journal. Here are some suggestions for questions to ask yourself each week to monitor your progression toward your goals.

As you review the questions, strive to be as honest with yourself as possible. The plan works only if you are guided by your conscience and self-awareness and a deep desire to achieve goals and pursue a vision that is in line with your most heartfelt beliefs, values, and principles. In other words, you can't effectively pursue something that you really don't want, and you can't become someone you don't want to be. It all comes from within.

- Which activities moved you most effectively toward your goals?
- What difficulties did you have?
- How did you deal with these difficulties?
- Which activities were beneficial and which weren't?
- Did having scheduled activities help you stay focused and motivated?
- Were you able to coordinate family activities with work or community activities?
- What beliefs, values, or principles came into play during the week?

- Were any of those beliefs, values, or principles challenged, compromised, or set aside?
- How does this week measure up against others as far as activities that moved you toward your goals?
- Do your goals and your vision for your life still appear to be realistic? Challenging? Worthy?
- Are you asking too much of yourself? Not enough?
- Is there any problem or obstacle that seems to be appearing on a regular basis?
- Is there anything about your plan that needs improvement? Your motivation?

## STAYING FOCUSED ON YOUR DREAMS

You have probably seen photographs of carriage horses in Central Park in New York, along Michigan Avenue in Chicago, or in other cities around the world. Many of them wear blinders that allow them to see only where they are supposed to be going. The blinders block out distractions so that they keep on going in the right direction: that is what you need to do in pursuing your dreams. There are several key points to remember when you set out to pursue your vision for your life.

Rule No. 1: *It is just as important to know what not to do as what to do.* It is important not to back down when faced with challenges or hard times as you follow your vision, but it is equally important that you don't waste time on things you cannot control. You have to leave alone those things that you cannot control and focus on the things that you can change in order to achieve your goals.

Problems outside your control generally are related to something that has happened in the past or something involving your current circumstances. You can influence only your current and future behavior, so you should not waste your time fretting over something that is in the past. This is reflected in the Serenity Prayer: *God grant me the power to accept the things that I cannot change, the courage to change the things I can, and the wisdom to know the difference.*

Rule No. 2: *Don't allow yourself to be distracted from the truly important things in your journey by the* urgent *things that cry out to you.* For example, it might be *important t*hat you get your master's thesis done within a few days, so you have to put off the *urgent* things such as a car that won't start, telephone calls to relatives, and laundry piling up in the closet.

When important things and urgent things coincide in your journey through life, there is often a crisis as a result. This is sometimes unavoidable, but if you spend too much time managing crises, you'll become stressed out, burned out, and worn out. Former U.S. Secretary of State Henry Kissinger said, "Next week there can't be any crisis. My schedule is already full." He was obviously aware that too often things that appear urgent are not important, even though they might appear to be. The ringing phone might have an urgent sound to it, but it's as likely to be a telemarketing salesperson or a gossipy friend as it is to be something that is really important to your life and your journey toward your goals.

Rule No. 3: *Don't procrastinate.* Putting things off is a terrible habit that is the result of not staying focused on what is truly important. I inherited the tendency to put things off from my mother. I used to always say, "I'll get to it later." Things would pile up on me and opportunities would get lost because I procrastinated. This tendency really hit home a few years ago when I was applying for a grant for Athletes Against Drug and I kept putting off filling out the forms. One of the people administering the grant kept telling me that I'd better get it submitted, but I didn't pay attention. As a result, I didn't get the grant, and it was a good one. Since then, I've worked on doing things as they come to me, rather than putting them aside.

Procrastination is a by-product of fear. It is a protective mechanism for those who want to stay within a certain comfort zone. It is very detrimental to any kind of advancement. By making the wrong decisions during the course of a day, you waste time. Make too many wrong decisions and life will pass you by. You will feel stuck. And unless you start making the right decisions, you will *be* stuck. If you skip your workout today, if you go play tennis rather than working on your résumé, if you keep resetting the alarm clock, then remember this: *You snooze, you lose.*

Rule No. 4: *Every day, do something that is truly important in moving you toward your goals.* You must choose to invest your time in the important steps. When you take charge of your time, you take charge of your life. How you spend your time reflects your priorities. When you have trouble taking the steps to reach a goal, you need to explore whether the goal really reflects your deepest needs, desires, and values—your true priorities in life.

## PREPARING YOURSELF FOR THE SUCCESS PROCESS

Once you have a plan for your journey with routes to specific stops along the way to your ultimate destination, it is important to check and see if you are packed properly. Are you fully prepared to begin the Success Process? Having a vision and goals and a plan to reach them is essential, but you have to make sure that you are properly prepared to begin your journey and to undertake it in a manner that is consistent with the principles and beliefs that you have chosen to guide your life.

When you are taking actions to reach your goals, you must always keep an eye on what is most important to you, so that in the process of going after your goals you don't get off track as a person. Remember that in pursuing your vision you have to also look after your physical health and your overall well-being. Your financial health is vital, but you need to monitor your mental and spiritual health as well.

We all have read stories and heard reports of people who have chased fame and fortune and gotten it, only to have their lives fall apart because they neglected other important aspects of their lives, so that when success came, they couldn't handle all that came with it—the notoriety, the responsibility, the demands on their time. This happens to people outside the limelight too. I know of a man who grew up in the Midwest, fought in Vietnam, and then came home and started off in business as a traveling salesman. Within a short time, he saw the opportunity to start his own business. He invited a friend to join him as a partner and together they built a multimillion-dollar manufacturing business. Without formal educations or any serious money in the bank, they created several businesses and profited beyond their wildest dreams.

But along the way, he lost his perspective. Making money and buying things became his total focus, to the extent that he neglected his relationships. He lives now in a mansion on his own estate, but there is a great deal of bitterness and hurt where there was once love and support. You can't buy those things. What a horrible feeling it would be to accomplish a goal or realize a dream and then to look at yourself and realize that you have been so focused on where you were going that you lost sight of what you had become. What if you achieved your goal to become the best salesman in your company, only to discover that you'd neglected your health so badly that you could no longer continue working? What if you fulfilled your vision of getting your master's degree, but had no one to share the victory with because in your march to that goal, you neglected your relationships, your friends and family? In the next chapter, I am going to offer you some "traveling gear" designed to help you stay on track and in touch as you journey through the Success Process.

# Chapter 5
# Master the Rules of the Road

>>>>>>>>>>>>>>>>>>>

*If there is no struggle, there is not progress.*

FREDERICK DOUGLASS

MY FRIENDS TELL a story about me that is painful to recall, but it says something about my determination, or my bullheadedness. Before we started dating, I used to water-ski quite a bit and I'd often told Oprah how much I enjoyed it. She said she would like to see me do it sometime, and the opportunity came on a trip to Florida. Now, I had talked my water-skiing talents way up, and I wanted to be able to dance, if not walk, on that water. The problem was, I didn't have my custom-made slalom ski with me. I had to have a special one because the standard ones don't fit my size 15 foot.

Without any choice, I squeezed into the slalom ski that was provided, but I had a great deal of difficulty getting up behind the ski boat because of the smaller ski. How much difficulty? I tried fifteen times and couldn't do it. I was out there on the water—make that *in* the water—for hours. The guy driving the boat told Oprah that he had never seen anyone so determined. Oprah told him: "If he doesn't get up he will keep trying until he dies,

so you had better do whatever you can to get him up on that ski."
She was right. I insisted that the boat driver keep trying. Meanwhile, Oprah was in the boat praying, "Oh Lord, please let him make it this time so we can go home!"

Even then, I didn't want to quit. But my arms became so sore they were actually swollen. I was really angry with myself for not making it up on the borrowed ski—so angry that I made everyone go back with me the next day to try again, and again, and again. It took twenty-three attempts before I finally made it up and water-skied. If I hadn't made it, we might still be out there.

My water-skiing story illustrates a very simple but important rule that I follow. If you want something in life you have to keep at it. Every time you fail, try again. If you fall down twenty-two times, go for twenty-three. You have to keep on keeping on when you are pursuing your dreams and goals. It is *always* too early to quit. That could be the motto for the Graham family. I come from a group of very determined people. Both my father and mother worked hard to support our family. My mother, Mary Graham, has dedicated herself to giving my younger brothers as normal a life as they could have. She worked from 11 P.M. until 7 A.M. for many years so she could be home with them when they most needed her, and she has won awards for her dedication to mental health organizations. My father, Stedman Sr., was relentless in working to provide for us all. He was primarily a house painter, but in the winter when it was too cold to paint, he would do tree trimming. He would often take me with him to help, and we would work from dawn until ten o'clock at night, cutting up branches. We would have to rig lights in the trees so we could see what we were doing.

Usually, I would have to brace the ladder from below while Dad was high on it working in the tree branches. With him relying on me to hold the ladder, I couldn't just take off for a coffee break. I had to hang in there with him. Believe me, you learn determination and perseverance standing at the bottom of a ladder for hours and hours in the cold, knowing that if you give up, your father might come crashing down to the ground! That is a powerful motivation, the sort you need to get any task done. As author Stephen Covey points out, the word *discipline* is derived from *disciple*, one who is devoted to something or someone. If you set goals and make plans you are on the right path, but if you aren't devoted to them, if you give up when the going gets tough or if you fall apart in the face of obstacles or opposition, you'll get nowhere.

## PACKING FOR YOUR JOURNEY TO A BETTER LIFE

In preparing you for your journey to a better life, so far we have looked at these steps in the Success Process:

- Increase your self-awareness so that you are in control of emotions and feelings that may have held you back in the past.
- Create a vision of your dreams and goals.
- Develop a plan to pursue those goals

In this chapter, I am going to tell you what vital characteristics you need to pack for your journey. Among those items you will need are self-discipline, determination, and perseverance to keep after your goals because there will always be distractions and disruptions in your journey to fulfill your vision of your life. You will also need to come up with your own personalized version of the *Rules of the Road* to keep your entire life on track as you travel this sometimes difficult road.

I learned while playing basketball that you never get to just go out on the court and play the game. It's not that easy in sports, or life. You never get to just do your thing. You always have to deal with difficulties and the opposition too. Someone or something is always testing your determination or standing in your path. If an opposing player challenges you and you show weakness, then he takes the advantage. But if you meet the challenge and keep fighting, you may lose, but at least you remain in the game and keep the dream alive that one day you'll have another opportunity to prove yourself.

"Everybody should have a dream," said Jesse Owens, the grandson of a slave and son of an Arkansas sharecropper. "Everybody should work toward that dream. And if you believe hard enough, whether it be in the Olympic Games, or be in the business world, or the music world or the educational world, it all comes down to one thing. One day we can all stand on the top of the victory stand, and one day we can watch our flag rise above all others to the crescendo of our national anthem, and one day, you can say, on this day, 'I am a champion.'"

Jesse Owens began working in the cottonfields and picking a hundred pounds of cotton a day at the age of seven, and so he knew a little bit about determination long before he became an Olympic athlete. He won four gold medals in the 1936 Olympics, in Germany, as Adolf Hitler watched on, perhaps wondering how a black man from Arkansas could defeat his supposed "superior race."

## DETERMINATION OVERCOMES ADVERSITY

Life responds to people like Jesse Owens, champions who never quit striving for their goals and dreams. And eventually, if you hang in there through the hard times and challenges, life will present you with opportunities to succeed. I'm reminded of a poster I saw recently. It had a photograph of a battered old rowboat stuck on a sandbar in the ocean. It was pretty forlorn looking with its oars sticking up in the air. But the caption on the photograph was full of hope. *The tide always turns*, it said.

It's true. If you hang in there and keep striving, most of the time the tide, and even tyranny, will turn. I have witnessed this in my life, and in the lives of many others too. Perhaps the greatest example in modern times of the power of perseverance was the triumph of Nelson Mandela over apartheid in South Africa. Here was a man who had spent decades in prison because he dared to demand that his people be treated equally in their own nation.

I was blessed to personally meet and speak with this great man shortly after his release from prison after twenty-six years. I had met Mandela's family through a mutual friend who has business interests in South Africa. When it became known that Mandela was going to be freed, Oprah and I agreed to help his family members living in Boston return to their homeland once it was deemed safe. I accompanied Mandela's daughter, Zenani, and other family members on their return to their homeland. It was an experience I will never forget.

On February 11, 1990, hundreds of Africans had waited peacefully outside the gates of the Victor Verster Prison. A string of cars slowly came from within the prison grounds toward the gates. A silver sedan came right to the front entrance, stopped, and a slight, gray-haired man in a dark suit stepped out. I was watching then, from Chicago, thousands of miles away, but I had the same impression that I would have a few days later when I actually met him in person. I remember thinking that he seemed like such an unassuming, ordinary man, full of dignity and quiet but obvious strength. This was a lion who did not need to roar.

As Mandela spoke to the crowd on the day of his release, his delivery was very low-key. But his words were powerful. At first, he just looked into the sky, then he turned his gaze to the people in front of him and he raised one clenched fist, then the other into the air. The crowd cheered but he did not speak there. He got back into the car for a motorcade through Cape Town. The streets were lined with thousands of supporters. At one point, three traffic policemen requested his autograph, and Mandela gave it to them, signing their ticket books. It seemed like everyone in the world, black, white, or otherwise, was Mandela's friend that day.

Two days later in Soweto, more than 100,000 people had waited all day at the Grand Parade Stadium to hear his words as a freed man. What struck me was that after all those years of being imprisoned, taunted, and terrorized because of his dream for a free South Africa, Mandela was still fighting for what he believed in. He had won the respect of even his opponents, to the point that some were cheering and asking for his autograph that day. He called upon his followers to not let up their fight for freedom simply because he had been released. "Seize the moment," he told them, "so that the process towards democracy is rapid and uninterrupted. We have waited too long for our freedom. We can no longer wait. Now it the time to intensify the struggle on all fronts."

Mandela was well-equipped for his journey. He possessed so much inner strength and determination that he made admirers of his jailers. Through the strength of his will, he forced the white power structure of South Africa to release him from prison. Even then, he kept on pursuing his dream of a free South Africa. Instead of retiring to a comfortable life, which he has surely earned, Mandela fought for free elections and for the top leadership position in the very nation that had tried to enslave him and his people.

My respect for him grew with every word I heard that day and it continued to expand during those days when I had the opportunity to observe him closely. I had breakfast and tea with Mandela and his family just a few days after his release. He had been conducting interviews with the media for days but he seemed to draw strength from the air around him. He was so humble, very direct in what he had to say, and deeply principled. He was extremely grateful to us for bringing the family members back to him, and he was warm and loving to them.

"What was it like to be imprisoned for so long for such a powerful cause?" I asked him. He said it had not been pleasant being away from family and loved ones for so long, and he noted that they had been forced to carry on without him. I think people forget how much Winnie Mandela had to go through during her husband's imprisonment. Though some have vilified her, I found her to be an extraordinary woman. She too had been imprisoned and tortured and relentlessly harassed by the upholders of apartheid. She dealt with that for years and years and years, and although she is not perfect, she kept the struggle alive, and for that the people of South Africa should be grateful. Her strength and perseverance are to be admired too, for without her, Mandela's message might have died.

Nelson Mandela's spirit proved so powerful that on election day in South Africa, he won the vote of even the grandson of the white leader who had been known as "the architect of apartheid." Mandela became the head of a nation that had imprisoned him, and on his inaugural day he proclaimed, "Let freedom reign." He proved that if you refuse to be broken, you cannot be enslaved. If there is any greater example of the power of determination, I do not know of it. It is extraordinary.

As Mandela showed us, life is a journey we travel one day at a time. Day by day and step by step, you have to maintain your vigilance and hold on to your vision for your life, no matter what happens around you or to you. To get where we want to go in life, we have to keep at it. We have to create a vision, make choices based on what moves us most swiftly toward our goals, and go after them with determination and single-mindedness. And whenever you encounter a problem, no matter how insurmountable it might seem, there is one simple response that should be ingrained in your behavior. Never give up.

Jesse Owens and Nelson Mandela became heroes around the world for their determination and triumphs, but every day people show remarkable courage and determination in their quiet struggles for better lives too. I'll wager most folks have never heard of Unita Blackwell of Lula, Mississippi, but she did for her state something that was, in its way, equal to what Mandela did for his nation.

Mrs. Blackwell became the mayor of Meyersville, Mississippi, in 1976, which made her the first black mayor in Mississippi history, and it put her in charge of the very city where she had been harassed by the police for her civil rights advocacy. During one period, before she ran for public office, she was arrested every day for thirty days straight. Her cars were turned upside down, crosses were burned in her yard, and homemade bombs were thrown at her house because she fought for civil rights and voter registration for African Americans in the Deep South.

Unita Blackwell was one very ordinary yet very heroic and very determined woman. She had no idea that she and her fellow activists were helping change a nation by fighting for civil rights in the 1960s, she once said. She was merely determined to make a better life for herself and for her family. "We were doing it because we didn't have shoes for our children and decent houses to stay in and just the everyday life that we wanted," Mrs. Blackwell told an interviewer a few years ago.

This woman, who obtained a master's degree from the University of Massachusetts in 1983 at the age of fifty, serves as proof that if you have the determination to fight for what you want, you can create a better life.

Jesse Owens, Nelson Mandela, and Unita Blackwell never lost sight of what they were pursuing. They were determined, disciplined, and they persevered. Before you set out on your own journey, it would be wise to check and see if you have all of the tools and gear that may be required. Before putting your plan for bettering your life into action, you need to be prepared in every aspect of your life—the physical, the social, the mental, and the spiritual.

## YOUR PHYSICAL HEALTH

Your physical well-being is vital if you are to effectively pursue a better life. You must take care of your body by exercising, eating well, and getting adequate rest. If you don't do those things, you might hide your poor health for a while, but eventually your physical health will deteriorate and affect the other facets.

It is extremely difficult to concentrate mentally on tasks when your physical heath is deteriorating. Relationships also suffer when you are in poor health, and focusing on your spiritual growth is also a challenge. When you dedicate a portion of each day to building your physical health, it builds energy and a sense of empowerment. I work out nearly every day for several hours, playing tennis, racquetball or basketball, lifting weights, jogging, and I really look forward to it. If I miss even a day, I grow lethargic. I can feel my body weaken. Being physically healthy adds a great deal to every other aspect of your life. If you have never been in great shape, it should become one of your priorities, a major goal. You should exercise at a steady pace to get your heart rate up at least thirty minutes a day. Once you start, you will wonder how you ever let yourself slide. I promise you, it will change your life.

In the space below write down some things you can do to make sure that as you pursue your goals and your vision, you take care also of your body and your health.

To ensure my physical health I will:

_____

_____

_____

## Your Social Health

Your social well-being is centered on the quality of your relation-ships. That quality is largely dependent on whether or not people trust you and your motives. It is sad, but there are now all sorts of toll-free numbers and Internet chat rooms available to people who are lonely and lacking real ties to other people. For many people, these are nothing more than modern lonelyhearts clubs because they have been unable, for whatever reasons, to make a connection and establish real relationships.

There is no substitute for real social interaction; all people need it. Nor is there any substitute for the qualities it takes to build relationships. You can fake charm, you can smile and be a smooth talker, but eventually you have to prove your integrity, your trustworthiness, and your sincerity. To exist without love and trust and mutual support is to live a hollow life. If you feel that your social health is not what it should be, I suggest that you consider joining a club or special interest group that appeals to you. One of the best ways for shy people to meet others is to volunteer for charity work so that the focus is on helping others rather than on forced social interaction. You cannot deny the basic human needs to interact with others.

To insure my social health I will:

_____

_____

_____

_____

## Your Mental Health

Your mental well-being is maintained through continual learning and growth but it is fueled by a positive, optimistic approach to living. The next time you go to a class reunion, a large family reunion, or any big gathering of people, look to see where most of the energy is focused. Generally, it will be centered upon those people who have attained a high level of success through a positive mental approach to their own life's journey.

The people with the opposite form of energy, the negative, pessimistic types, will generally be found off in their own corner, or sitting alone. If you listen, you'll hear them grumbling about how life has done them wrong.

People who are actively engaged in the Success Process have a hunger for knowledge and a keen awareness of what is going on in the world around them. They read books, magazines, and newspapers to stay on top of the issues of the day. They may not be masters of technology, but they have a solid grasp of where it is headed and where the opportunities lie. They travel for recreation and also for self-education. They ask questions more often than they offer answers. They form their opinions based on as much information they can gather rather than on pure emotion or knee-jerk reaction.

Obviously, you cannot pursue a better life without being in good mental health with an alert mind. For a time, it was considered a cliché to urge people to *be optimistic* in their mental approach, but that has changed. Increasingly, serious researchers are finding that an optimistic attitude is every much as important as a high IQ in predicting an individual's ability to achieve his or her goals and dreams.

These researchers have found that people with a pessimistic approach to life tend to believe that bad things are inevitable, that they somehow triggered them, and that the problem will last a long time, undermining all of their plans. This negative attitude feeds on itself and fosters depression. Pessimists focus on the problems that they feel they face.

A person with an optimistic mental attitude, on the other hand, tends to view bad times as temporary, failure as a step to eventual success, and misfortune as the result of circumstances beyond his or her control. Optimists focus on solutions that they feel await their discovery.

If you feel your mental health is hindered by pessimism, I'd suggest you break the habit first by focusing on a solution. There are many books now that offer advice on how to train yourself to be more optimistic in your approach to life. It might also help to develop relationships with solution-oriented, positive, and optimistic people.

To insure my mental health I will:

---

---

---

## YOUR SPIRITUAL HEALTH

Your *spiritual* well-being begins with how you feel about yourself but it does not end there. It runs much deeper into the realm of how you relate to others, respond to others, and what you bring into the lives of others. It is a connection between your public persona and your innermost thoughts on what matters most in your life. Having a solid spiritual base promotes self-discipline, an inner calm, and an ability to love others as much as you love yourself—all of which are essential gear in the journey to a better life.

Understand, though, that your life has a spiritual quality only when it is based on something other than self. Animals live for themselves. Humans, hopefully, live to serve something greater than the individual. Organized religion is a primary method to build spiritual health, but there are many other ways, including the study of ancient philosophies. Some people build spiritual health by reading Scriptures, some by meditating in a darkened room, some by sitting on the beach basking in nature's beauty,

some by listening to beautiful music, reading powerful literature, or looking at great works of art.

There are those, also, who act as though this aspect of human
existence has no relevance to their lives, and it is true, it is possible to achieve your goals without having a healthy spiritual life.
Whether or not you can fully appreciate and enjoy those successes without a spiritual base is another matter.

To insure my spiritual health I will:

_____

_____

_____


## REALIZING ALL THINGS ARE CONNECTED

All aspects of your existence—physical, social, mental, and spiritual—are interrelated. If you neglect one area, eventually the
others will suffer. Mental stress and anxiety, for example, can
trigger physical illness. They can do as much harm to your body
as any virus by robbing you of restful sleep and proper digestion
and inhibiting your natural resistance. Medical scientists now
believe that stress can accelerate the spread of cancer, make you
more susceptible to viral attack, and trigger asthma, ulcers, coli-
tis, colds, and the flu. Being under stress is also thought to increase the risk of blocked arteries.

On the other hand, if one of the four aspects of your life is troubled, the others can be used to help it heal if they are strong. If
you are knocked down by a physical ailment, you can call upon
your spiritual beliefs—your religious faith, your faith in your
own goodness and the goodness of those around you—to help
you get through the sickness, just as you can also call upon your
mental strength and your social network of friends and family.

For me personally, it is beneficial to believe in God and to be able to turn to Him as a source of strength in times of need. My strong spiritual beliefs have gotten me through many hard times. Every day I say a prayer of thankfulness for the blessings bestowed upon me and I also ask for guidance. Everyone has their own way of building strength; it is a very personal thing.

In developing your plan for acting on your goals, then, it is important to understand how each of the four areas of need is connected to the other. By tending to all of them, you can find a path to your goals that will keep you balanced, fulfilled, and happy in your journey. If you neglect any one of them you run the risk of falling off the path, or going off in a direction that will not be as fulfilling or joyous for you.

## CHECKING YOUR GEAR

Fortunately, we all come fully equipped with essential tools to help us as we endeavor to make our way successfully in this world. Each of us has a *conscience*, a *will*, and the power of *imagination* to tap when we formulate our plans for acting upon our goals and pursuing a vision. How you apply each of these tools is crucial.

### LET YOUR CONSCIENCE BE YOUR GUIDE

Your *conscience* is the inner voice that serves as a quality-control check on your actions. Your conscience says: *Is this what I should be doing? Why am I doing this? Is this what I'm really all about?* It monitors your actions and attempts to keep them in line with your belief system. Recently, there was a story in the newspapers about a Midwestern farmer whose son was nearly ripped apart in a farming accident; all of his limbs and most of his scalp were torn off, though one arm, both legs, and portions of the scalp were reattached. He was badly mangled, but somehow the boy survived. The family had no insurance, however, and the medical bills were more than $500,000. After the newspaper story and other media accounts of the family's crisis appeared around the country, nearly 100,000 people responded by sending donations to them.

The farmer accepted most of the donations, which were generally in the $5 to $25 range, but he turned down several in the $10,000 to $20,000 range because he felt it was too much to take. Once he saw that his son's medical bills were going to be paid, he began sending checks back to people, thanking them, and explaining that the family was now able to take care of itself. That farmer's conscience was engaged. He was living out of his belief system rather than allowing himself to be seduced by greed or the power of material things.

How do you develop your conscience and learn to tune into it effectively as you develop a plan to pursue your vision? Some people read the Bible, others turn to the works of great philosophers and thinkers. It is also useful to keep a journal; that encourages you to record and monitor your experiences and your thought processes. Keeping a daily journal increases your self awareness and it also allows you to go back and track changes in how you view the world. Another benefit of a personal journal is that it often records the inner voices that you may otherwise tune out in day-to-day living. Of course, simply listening to your conscience isn't enough. You have to act upon that inner voice and mirror its instructions rather than following social trends or peer pressure. Following your conscience builds integrity.

## TAP INTO YOUR WILLPOWER

Your *will* gives you the power to respond to your conscience rather than to outside influences and distractions. The farmer might have been tempted to take all the money that was donated, but he had the will to act instead upon his conscience. You might feel compelled to talk about someone behind his or her back or to buy something you can't afford, but your conscience sounds the alert and your will gives you the power to choose what is most compatible with your belief system. Your will, then, helps you overcome your moods and fleeting desires to keep you on track for a life of integrity. Your will also keeps you going even when the going gets tough, because it holds you to your long-term vision, blocking out short-term distractions.

You can add muscle to your willpower by working hard at keeping your promises, both those you make to yourself, and those you make to others. Stephen Covey writes that if you want to learn to keep promises, you must first keep them to yourself. Every time you fail to do something that you said you would do, you reduce your value, and eventually, your *brand name* will lose its value in the market. If you take promises seriously you won't promise much, but those promises that you make will be kept. To work out that strength, promise yourself you are going to lose five pounds, and then do it. Promise yourself you are going to get a half-hour of exercise every day of the week, and then do it. Promise yourself you are going to read up on a special interest for at least an hour every day, and do it. By living up to these small promises, you build your strength to fulfill larger ones and you build confidence in your ability to control your own life rather than submitting to the control of others, or blaming outside influences for what happens in your life.

When I look back on my early life, I see that I made promises easily, but it was usually in the moment, and I didn't honor those promises as I should have, because I didn't put enough weight on keeping my word. Now, in business, it is necessary to make commitments and follow through, or I won't be in business long.

## INGENIOUS ACTIONS

It is also necessary to be imaginative in planning actions to achieve your goals. Your *ingenuity* allows you to keep your goals in mind, to see ahead, beyond your present situation and circumstances, to the day when you will have fulfilled your vision for your life. It also helps you to search for and find *ingenious* solutions to problems that you will encounter along the way. Like a Sherlock Holmes, who finds clues where others see nothing out of the ordinary, people who tap into ingenuity find solutions where others only see problems. People who live out of their imaginations do the ordinary things, and if they don't work, they do extraordinary things to make them work.

By using your ingenuity, you can learn to visualize yourself responding to problems, challenges, and bad situations in a more positive and productive manner by tapping into the imagination, and then using your will to choose that response over one driven by your emotions or moods. The best way to determine your own destiny is to control it and create it. This is a part of what true freedom is all about.

## ENGAGING YOUR RULES OF THE ROAD

Before putting into action your plans for pursuing a better life, you need to complete one more task by preparing your own version of the Rules of the Road. That is the guidebook you get when you receive your driver's license or when you take the test for renewal of your license. It tells you what the traffic laws are in your state, and identifies the road signs.

I would like you to create Rules of the Road that establish guidelines for how you will travel along the Success Process. These rules should be based on the values and principles that you have chosen to guide your life. They are to be guidelines to help you stay on the true course to your goals and give you the strength and determination to fight and overcome distractions, hardships, and obstacles. You know that Jesse Owens, Nelson Mandela, and Unita Blackwell were all sorely tested in their pursuit of better lives. Owens was taunted by armed Nazis. Mandela was beaten and placed in a former leper colony. Mrs. Blackwell was thrown in jail repeatedly.

How did they persevere? How did they stay focused? How did they not lose their way? At one point during his imprisonment, Mandela was offered a deal by his jailers. If he would renounce his call for majority rule and go quietly into retirement, he could go free. He had already made his point, his jailers argued. No one would blame an old man for wanting to go home. But he refused. He said he would rather stay in jail than sell out his principles.

Mandela had very well-defined rules for the road. Most of us, whether consciously or unconsciously, live our lives within guidelines or principles that have stood the test of time, concepts as simple but as lasting as the Golden Rule: *Do unto others as you would have them do unto you.*

These principles are present in many religions, but they are not necessarily religious. Often, they are long-standing and proven truths, present in the teachings of many great philosophers, gurus, wise men, saints, and historic figures, ranging from Moses to Joan of Arc, to Henry David Thoreau, to the Dalai Lama. Think of them as your personal Rules of the Road—guidelines for a life of quality and integrity. If you stand by them, you are more likely to be successful in *all* aspects of your life—physically, socially, mentally, spiritually, and professionally.

Your personal Rules of the Road are, in a sense, much like the laws that govern nature. Everything in nature is related to everything else; natural laws cannot be denied. As much as you might like to, you can't skip winter and go directly from fall to spring. If you eat junk food constantly, nature is going to take its toll on your body and your overall health. If you defy the principles that most of humankind has followed over the ages, you will not succeed in your quest for a better life. It is that simple. Oh, you may accomplish some of your goals; you may even better your life to some degree. It happens. But what kind of person will you have become?

Your responses to the circumstances that life presents you are rooted in your habits. As long as your vision for your life is a true expression of your deeply held values, needs, and desires, you should be able to resolve conflicts over priorities—choosing the important steps—and stay on track in the Success Process. If you have a great deal of difficulty staying on course, it is likely that your goals are not really consistent with your deeply held values.

I'd like you to come up with five Rules of the Road that guide your life, but first I'll offer a list of my own as an example. Mine are simple, but they are based on time-tested principles.

## 1. BE HONEST

As someone who always tries to build value in his life, I believe that you have no value to other people if they can't believe what you say. Trust is built on perceptions of honesty. Throughout my life I have known people whom I have enjoyed being with but whom I did not fully trust, and so the relationships did not go very far. None of us are perfect. Even when our intentions are good, sometimes we can't always do what we say we are going to do. But if you are honest with people even when you fail, you at least maintain your credibility over time.

## 2. DO THE WORK THAT IS REQUIRED

What you put into any project or plan or endeavor is reflected in how it turns out. Why waste your time doing something halfheartedly? I'm guilty sometimes of spreading myself too thin, but as I become a more mature businessman, I realize that it is far more satisfying to take on fewer tasks and concentrate on doing them well.

You know in your heart what you need to do to realize your goals. If you do less, it only hurts you. I am sure the Olympic runner would just as soon cut a couple of miles off his training route each day, but he knows that doing less will hurt his performance. Don't make excuses. Do the work that is required.

## 3. MAINTAIN A POSITIVE ATTITUDE

Being positive begins with eliminating the negative. That includes negative thoughts in your mind, negative relationships, anything that interferes with your ability to move forward. I had one of my family members call my administrative assistant recently about the family reunion that I am hosting, and make threats. This family member has abused our relationship in the past. I was tempted to call this person back and let him have it, but I decided to leave that negative energy untapped. Sometimes the best way to take the power away from a negative person is to just ignore him or her.

## 4. TAKE THE TIME TO THINK THINGS THROUGH

We have a wonderful capacity to think, but too often we submit to the temptation to act without giving enough thought beforehand. So much of what we do is *react* because immediate action gives more instant gratification, but if you develop a pattern of thinking about what you are doing first, you eliminate many errors and crises. Those who take time to think and plan out their lives are the ones who get the greatest benefit out of whatever they are involved in.

## 5. Look at the Big Picture

Too many people think first from the point of "me." That is small-picture thinking. If you look at the big picture, your thought processes revolve around how you can make a difference in the lives of others. Looking at the big picture also gives you perspective on how your actions and words will impact those around you. When you operate from this perspective, you offer leadership to those around you, and being a leader attracts greater opportunities to you.

## YOUR RULES OF THE ROAD

In the space below, write your own Rules of the Road to help guide the way you live. Review them often so that you stay on track.

1. _____

   _____

2. _____

   _____

3. _____

   _____

4. _____

   _____

5. _____

   _____

Refer to your Rules of the Road as you take action on your goals. Check them if you feel your life has lost balance. Keep in mind also that while you should be goal-oriented, it is important not to lose sight of the things you value in life. Remember the key questions: What kind of person do you want to be at the end of your life's journey? What do you want your legacy to be to your family? What will people say about you when you are gone? I think Stephen Covey would have to agree that when you consider those thoughts you are certainly beginning with the *real end* in mind.

I always advise people to *clean the windshield* before you set out for your goals. By that, I mean for you to make sure you can clearly see where you want to go, that your vision for your life is not in any way blurred or distorted. It's all too easy for that to happen as you go through life. I'm sure you know people whose vision of their lives has been affected by anger, hurt, materialism, grief. Your weekly review of your progress toward your goals should also include a period of time when you step back off the path and, again, clean the windshield to make sure that you are living according to the beliefs, principles, and values that you most want to guide your life.

How does this approach work in day-to-day living? Say that tomorrow you go to work and:

- The deadline on your current project just got moved up two weeks.
- Your most valuable co-worker got transferred.
- There are a dozen urgent messages demanding your attention.
- And your spouse calls to say one of the children is sick at school and needs a ride home.

Now, you might easily be tempted to follow the standard practices of prioritizing, postponing, delegating, ignoring, rearranging, and dodging. All are time-honored methods of crisis management. But where do they get you?

Instead, by stepping back and viewing the demands on your time from a deeper perspective, you may be able to deal with solutions rather than the problems. Why was the deadline moved up? Will the change result in improved service or product to the customer or client? Is this way of doing business in line with the company's mission, goals, and values? And are the company's mission, goals, and values in line with mine?

The key here is that instead of spending your time each day dealing with problems, it is far better to be *working on solutions*. This approach can be applied in family matters too. When my daughter was considering which college to attend and what to major in, we sat down together and instead of approaching it by considering the problems of location, costs, admission policies, and so forth, we focused instead on what her goals were for her life. I asked her, "*What do you want to be doing in ten years?*" And from that wider and deeper perspective, we worked together to find a college and determine a course of study that would get her where she wanted to be in ten years.

We didn't focus on which school would be the easiest to get into, or the least expensive, or the most fun. We didn't focus on individual classes or curriculums. We focused on what her vision of her life was, what her goals were, and then we developed a plan to carry that out.

When you keep your goals and your vision for your life in alignment with your rules for living, you don't get easily thrown off. You tend to see opportunities where others see problems. You seek cooperation and build relationships where others might prefer combat and confrontation. When you are *living large* you don't allow yourself to get beaten down and swept under by a system or the daily grind. You find ways to change that system and to transform the grind into a game you can win. You tend to view all of life as a success process, and you don't get easily frustrated or angry.

You tend to see problems as opportunities to exercise your talents and knowledge. You aren't afraid of challenges, because you see them as a stimulant to growth, just as a weightlifter sees the resistance he meets as a way to build strength. This also enables you to perceive differences in opinion with other people as natural and expected and valuable because those differences challenge you to understand and seek common ground.

## FULFILLING RESPONSIBILITIES ON THE ROAD

There is one last thing to consider before setting off on your journey. You can't leave your responsibilities at home. It is vital that you consider how your actions along the way will impact on all aspects of your life, on every relationship and responsibility that you have. Many of the conflicts in our lives come when we focus on one aspect of life but neglect another, when we work so hard at our jobs that we neglect our relationships, or when we focus on serving our customers without keeping an eye on the bottom line of the budget.

Each of us has many roles to fill. I am an employer, a board member, a partner in a relationship, a father, a son, a friend, a club member, among other roles. When I put together a plan for achieving my goals, I had to consider how my actions would impact each of those roles and how I could maintain harmony in each of them while pursuing my vision.

Consider all of your relationships, affiliations, and duties and then write down the roles that you fill:

Role 1. _____

Role 2. _____

Role 3. _____

Role 4. _____

Role 5. _____

Now, consider how much time you invest in each role and whether or not you neglect some roles because you dwell too much on the others. Weigh the importance of each role and whether or not they are all in harmony with your vision for your life. If not, there may be some roles you should consider eliminating. For instance, if you still serve on the advisory board to the YMCA, even though you are no longer a member, that may be a role you would consider eliminating in order to focus more on what is important in your life now.

The idea here is to show you that your roles are not necessarily mutually exclusive; in fact, they are usually interrelated, and so you can pursue your vision without neglecting any of your roles if you plan carefully and imaginatively. I have a friend who is a journalist. His work takes him all over the country, but he often takes family members with him so that he can spend time with them, and so that they see why he enjoys his work. He understands the importance of both roles and how they are interrelated.

When you review your roles, use your conscience to determine what is most important. And now list those roles again, and next to each of them write down your long-term goal within that role.

*Example: In my role as a father, I will pursue my vision of building a business so that my daughter might one day be a part of that business. Within the context of that, I will do my best to keep her informed of developments in my business and to nurture her interest in it.*

Role 1. _____

Goal: _____

Role 2. _____

Goal: _____

Role 3. _____

Goal: _____

Role 4. _____

Goal: _____

Role 5. _____

Goal: _____

To properly serve each of your roles in life, you have to maintain balance between them; between work and family, between
family and recreation, between recreation and education, between education and experience. Life is a process of continually
seeking balance, and the key to achieving balance is in realizing
that your roles are all interrelated. You don't have to give up
your family for your career. Not if you use your conscience and
imagination and willpower to devise a plan to pursue your vision that incorporates both career and family.

There will always be times, of course, when it is necessary to
focus on one role more than others, just as, if one of your children
is injured, that child naturally becomes the center of attention.
But at the same time, if that child's injury demands attention
over a long period, it is important to reach out to the other children to assure them that they are still important, and to bring
them in on the nurturing of the injured child. The key is to understand that even though your life will naturally run in cycles
that place the focus on one role over another from time to time,
over the long run, balance is essential.

There is nothing wrong, then, with devoting your attention to
pressing and urgent matters, as long as you remember that they
are only important *for the moment* and that there are other things
that are important *for a lifetime.*

## Chapter 6
# Step into the
# Outer Limits

*Some of us are timid. We think we have something to lose so we don't try for the next hill.*

MAYA ANGELOU

WHEN I WAS a boy, I watched some of the scariest shows on television: *Alfred Hitchcock Presents*, *The Twilight Zone*, and, maybe the scariest for me, *The Outer Limits*. I don't know why I watched those shows, because I'd have trouble getting to sleep after sitting through them with my hands over my eyes. For me, *The Outer Limits* was the scariest because of the way it always began, with the image on the television screen flickering and then turning into static, and this scary voice saying that control of your television set had been taken over for the next sixty minutes.

That opening sequence always fooled me for at least a few seconds. I grew up in an era in which television programming was interrupted all too often with very real and frightening news. The Cuban missile crisis, the assassinations of John and Robert Kennedy and Martin Luther King, and civil rights demonstrations and confrontations were among the most frightening events that were played out on television. News bulletins announcing great tragedies and unsettling civil unrest seemed to regularly interrupt our regular programming. It was disorienting, not to mention scary, for me as a child.

So the *Outer Limits* introduction was more disturbing back then than it might seem today, because of all the disorder in the real world. Although it triggers emotions different from those set off by a loud bang or a monster at the door, loss of control is a scary thing for most people. No one likes the thought of losing control, even when, in truth, the person may not really be in control in the first place. It is natural for people to want to stay with what is familiar and comfortable in their lives rather than for them to venture into the outer limits of the unknown. Most people want to stay within their *comfort zones*, where they feel safe and secure.

Fear of the unknown is one of the greatest obstacles that you will face when you are traveling the journey of the Success Process. But if you want a better life than that which you have now, you must learn to overcome that natural fear and to step outside what has become comfortable and familiar. You must risk losing control in order to push yourself into the outer limits of your abilities and talents. That is how you move to a higher level of achievement. It is the way to a better life.

Take a minute now to look at your life. Are you stuck in a comfort zone in any aspect of your life? Are you hanging on to a relationship or job simply because you are scared to look for something that would be more rewarding and more fulfilling? Don't misunderstand: there is nothing wrong with being happy and comfortable in a relationship or job that you truly love and find stimulating and fulfilling. On the other hand, I have known women who stayed with men who abused them physically or emotionally. Often they did not leave because their fear of the unknown was stronger than their fear of being hurt in the existing relationship. I've also known people who stayed in dead-end jobs that drained the life out of them because they preferred the security of a no-brainer job to the challenge of a potentially more energizing one.

Sometimes a person's comfort zone isn't even truly comfortable but the individual stays in it because he or she would rather deal with the *known* than the *unknown*. When that is the situation, the person's life is being guided by fear rather than hope, and that is no way to live. In fact, you are not really living when your fears control your actions. Instead, you are hiding from life.

## PUSHING YOURSELF AND YOUR TALENTS TO THE OUTER LIMITS

We are now halfway through the book and ready to step out on our journey to pursue a better life. We have prepared by looking at how you could:

- Increase your self-awareness so that you are in control of emotions and feelings that may have held you back in the past.
- Create a vision of your dreams and goals.
- Develop a plan to pursue those goals.
- Come up with your own Rules of the Road to stay focused on your plan without losing sight of the people and principles that are important to you.

As you proceed on your journey in pursuit of a better life, however, you may begin to feel uncomfortable because you are entering new terrain. Pursuing your dreams requires you to leave your established comfort zone and to push into areas where you may feel at first that you have less control. When you set out on your journey, you have to be willing to grow, to push your talents to the outer limits. That means pushing beyond what is known to you, taking risks, and learning to view failure as merely a step, rather than a defeat, in your journey along the Success Process.

Just as a tree grows by pushing buds up through the existing branches, you have to push yourself to grow beyond your current circumstances. This is where you have to walk the walk if you are serious about changing your life. It takes courage to take risks, to do things that we feel may expose us to the possibility of danger, loss, failure, or injury. Because of the potential for those negative outcomes, most people—outside of stuntmen and daredevils—avoid taking risks as much as possible. But can you really escape taking risks in life? What can we do that has no risk to it? Love our family? Stay in the house all day? Go to church?

The truth is that nothing is risk-free. Loving your children or family members involves the risk of losing them, or having them hurt you with their behavior, but no one would consider withholding love rather than incur that risk. Any relationship involves risk, but if you spend your whole life avoiding involvement because you don't want to get hurt, what sort of life will you have? A lonely one.

Staying in the house all day might seem like a good way to avoid risk, but insurance companies say that most accidents happen in the home. How many times have you read of someone being killed when an airplane crashes through the roof, or a car veers off the road into their living room? It happens. Even religious worship carries the risk of being persecuted or martyred in some areas of the world. There is no hiding from risk. Simply staying within your comfort zone, simply *doing nothing*, carries risk too.

It is important to regularly assess your position in life, to ask yourself whether you are moving forward, standing still, or even going backward in the Success Process. Again, this process refers not necessarily to financial or career success but to *living* a fully engaged life in which all of your gifts and talents are developed and put to their highest use.

To live a fulfilling life, you can't always cling to what is comfortable, not if you want to keep growing and bettering yourself. I'm not a kid anymore, but my comfort zone is still in sports. Although I haven't played professional basketball for more than twenty-five years, I still am more at home playing sports than anywhere else. I still love the competition, the exhilaration of physical exercise, and the camaraderie of sports. I have to admit, it feels great when I hear someone say, *"Stedman can still play the game."* Sports are definitely within my comfort zone. But it wasn't until I stepped out of the comfort of my athletic career that I saw the greater possibilities for my life. I could have continued to play basketball in Europe for many years but I knew that playing professional basketball was not something I could do forever. I was eager to grow.

## GETTING UNSTUCK

Too often we get comfortable at one level of achievement in our personal lives or jobs and then just kick back and coast. Then, before you know what hit you, you find yourself *stuck*. One morning you wake up, look around, and ask yourself, "What happened to my dream for my life? What about all those great things I was going to accomplish? All the adventures and dreams I had envisioned for my life? How did I get stuck?"

You get stuck by forgetting that life is a process of continual striving and challenge, of pushing your talents and knowledge. Sounds like work, doesn't it? That's why so many people get stuck. It's like setting out on a journey to the destination of your dreams, *Paradise Mountain*, but stopping along the way at a Comfort Inn and then never leaving. It's nice for a while at that inn. You've got a pool, room service, movies in the room, and a nice restaurant, but sooner or later you have to get back on the road if you are serious about reaching your original destination.

How do you know when you're stuck? Look around. Is your current situation what you had envisioned for your life? Do you get up in the morning *excited* about the potential for the day? When the phone rings, are you eager to find out who it is, what new development it might bring? Or do you resent the interruption and dread answering? At the end of your life, will you look back and say, *I used life up! I rode it all the way, I took all of my talents and abilities as far as they would go*? Or will you say, *I stopped too soon. I settled for the consolation prize instead of the grand prize*?

That's not to say that you can't find happiness somewhere other than the destination that you had originally set out for. It happens all the time. Life doesn't follow a set script. Remember the movie *Doc Hollywood*? In it, a young doctor, played by Michael J. Fox, sets out for California to be a plastic surgeon, but en route he gets delayed in a small Southern town, and eventually, in spite of himself, he finds love and fulfillment there. The young doctor in the movie tries to stick with his original dream, but when he checks his beliefs, values, and principles he discovers that the small-town family practice, and the woman he has fallen in love with, are much more in line with what he really values. That is why it is important to always use your values and principles as guidelines when you travel in the Success Process. If you are feeling stuck in your current situation, odds are that you are not living up to your expectations for your life.

*Oh yeah, well I've settled for a pretty nice life*, you might say. If you are content with your life, fine, but don't *settle* for anything. Don't compromise your goals and dreams. You may believe in reincarnation, but I haven't seen enough proof to convince me that I'm going to get another chance. I want to live this one to the fullest, so I don't want to *settle* for anything. I want to leave the planet with every last bit of my energy used up. I want all my gauges on empty, every talent and ability and interest exhausted.

There are people in my hometown, people my age, who were afraid to leave the security of their lives there. I'm sure you know similar people. You go home and run into them, and they have no more energy than the sidewalk. That's not to say that there are not people who stay in their hometowns and lead very good, meaningful, and fulfilling lives. Many people do; they find ways to energize their lives, and because of them, their communities continue to thrive. But others stay where they grew up because they are afraid to venture outside the comfortable and familiar. And too often they never seek to develop those talents at home. They never take life on. You don't necessarily have to change locations to do that. You can change the world with an idea even if you never leave your front porch. The late Sam Walton, the founder of Wal-Mart, never left Arkansas, yet he certainly had a powerful impact. The Success Process is really an inner journey and it requires a great deal of courage to take the risks that are often encountered along the way.

## THE RISKY BUSINESS OF LIFE

Each of us takes risks every day. You take physical risks getting on the highway, boarding an airliner, or jogging down the street. You take those risks knowingly, figuring the benefit is greater than the potential for danger. How about risk-taking in your personal life and your career? Sometimes, to go after a better life, you have to take calculated risks, whether that means trying a new job, leaving an unhealthy relationship, or offering yourself as a candidate for a community leadership position.

Identify two risks you have taken during the last year.

Risk A: _____

_____

Risk B: _____

_____

Now, select one of those risks and answer the following questions related to your decision to take that risk.

1.  Your goal in assuming this risk was:

———————————————————————————————

———————————————————————————————

———————————————————————————————

2.  Your backup plan if things did not work out was:

———————————————————————————————

———————————————————————————————

———————————————————————————————

3.  The people who supported you in taking this risk were:

———————————————————————————————

———————————————————————————————

———————————————————————————————

4.  Taking that risk resulted in:

———————————————————————————————

———————————————————————————————

———————————————————————————————

Risk-takers are courageous people with the mental and moral strength to take on their fears. That strength comes from a clear vision of what they want for their life and from a focus on their deepest values, needs, and desires. A clear vision and strong focus give them the power to pursue their goals in spite of fears and challenges.

Anthony Watson often thinks of the fears that nearly overwhelmed him as a boy growing up in Chicago's Cabrini-Green neighborhood, which is widely known today as one of the most violent in the country. In his childhood, it was not nearly as overrun with gangs and crime, but it was still a tough place. He often wondered whether he would grow up to take a place among the winos who populated a street corner near his family's apartment. He avoided alleys and even certain streets, where people he had known had lost their lives, and he paid protection dues to neighborhood bullies, giving them fifty cents to let him live another five minutes, or so they'd threaten.

Fears dominated his school days too. On his first day in the sixth grade at Cooley Upper Grade Center, an older boy spit on him. Yet, with the help of his parents, John and Virginia, Anthony faced his fears and overcame them. He became a good student and a standout football player, building confidence and courage that served him well after he earned an appointment to the United States Naval Academy in Annapolis, Maryland. But there too Anthony had to overcome hostility and his own fears as one of only a handful of urban blacks. He did it, reaching deep within for courage and strength, and he won over even classmates who had predicted he would never make it. In fact, they elected him president of their freshman class by a 98 percent majority. Now a veteran naval officer, there is little doubt that Anthony Watson will still have to face hostility and challenges in his life. That is to be expected, particularly when you are the commander of a nuclear-powered submarine. But there is no doubt that Commander Watson will be up to the challenges that await him.

Risk-takers believe in their ability to overcome obstacles and to solve problems. They have a *can do* attitude that is essential for taking risks. People with this attitude understand that failure is not the end of the road. They realize that in failure you can learn how to succeed and grow. The lessons we learn from things that don't work help us to discover those things that do work. It's been said that Thomas Edison had hundreds of failures before he finally came up with a lightbulb that worked. Yet, Edison didn't view those failures as defeats. He viewed them as steps in the process of success. "Results!" he once said. "Why, man, I have gotten a lot of results. I know several thousand things that won't work."

As a scientist, Edison understood that even failed experiments offered information that could eventually lead to success, but only if he kept working and trying and constantly evaluating his progress. "Many of life's failures are people who did not realize how close they were to success when they gave up," he said.

In taking risks, you will probably experience failures. It is up to you to decide whether those failures will become defeats, or whether they will lead to successes. When you learn to take risks and to view failure as part of the Success Process, you establish a pattern of continual growth. By living in this manner, you are always expanding your experience base, building on your strengths, and fortifying your self-confidence. That is why it is so important to learn to view failure as merely a lesson learned, a helpful marker that gives you a grasp for what you can and cannot do *at that point* in your life.

I love *Success* magazine, published by my friend Scott De-Garmo, and I recommend it to you as required reading along your journey because it is always full of stories about people who have pushed past their fears and defeats and created better lives for themselves. Recently the magazine reported on Ralph P. Gadiel of suburban Chicago, whose first business collapsed when he was fifty-two years old. He felt defeated, but then he read his daughter's college thesis, which dealt with *self-fulfilling prophecies*, or how people set their own course in life by creating goals and pursuing them with a positive attitude. His daughter's thesis inspired Gadiel to start a new business, International Resourcing Services Inc., which is a lofty-sounding name for a company that makes decorative porcelain miniature mining towns that are only three inches tall. Gadiel created a whole history of the collectible miniature town and wrote a book about it that he also sells. Within five years, his new business was generating revenues of $12 million, according to *Success*. And so, this man who had nearly given up at the age of fifty-two not only created a fictional village and a new business, he made a far better life for himself.

Identify someone you consider to be successful and ask that person how many failures he or she had before success came. I guarantee you that any successful person had to learn failure before success. That is what learning is all about. Doing it wrong to get it right. We don't all succeed at everything we try. Most of us go through failure to reach success, just as we go through fear in order to build courage. Ralph Waldo Emerson said, *"Do the thing you fear, and the death of fear is certain."*

Weightlifting is the simplest example I can think of to illustrate the process of going through failure to reach success. In fact, fitness instructors often talk about "going for failure." Now that sounds like fun, doesn't it? *Let's go fail!* What does that mean? In weightlifting, to go for failure means to push yourself to the limit; to lift as much as you can as many times as you can until you can't lift any more. Why do you do that? Fitness experts say that in order to build muscle, you first break it down, exhaust it, and then build new strength into it. By going for failure, you are preparing your muscles for greater success.

In weightlifting as in life, failure is nothing more than a part of the process of growing and building strength. You can't allow yourself to think of a failure as permanent. If you do that, you give failure too much power over your life. But if you put failure in its proper place, as simply a step in the Success Process, you empower yourself to take life on.

Can you think of a success that you have had that was built on a failure, or a series of failures? I can think of an example that most people share in their childhoods: learning how to ride a bike. How many times did you go out and try to ride that bike and fail? How many times did you skin your knees or bite the dirt? But each of those failures contributed to your eventual success, didn't they? (Don't tell me you still are riding around with the training wheels on.)

Write down a success that has come out of failure at some recent time in your life.

My success was: _____

Now, write down the failure(s) that preceded that success:

_____

_____

This exercise should help you in understanding that failure is not a finality, it is merely a step in the process and is not to be feared or dreaded. Look at one of the most successful athletes in history, Michael Jordan. He wasn't afraid of failure when he left basketball at the peak of his career and tried his skills at baseball. It was something he wanted to do with his life. He wanted to try and he wanted to succeed. But he didn't fear failure as some permanent condition. In fact, he did fail to make it as a professional baseball player, but I haven't heard anyone describe Michael as a loser or as a failure. He experienced failure, as we all do at one time or another, but he moved on with his dynamic life, looking for new challenges. This is why, in the second half of Jordan's basketball career, his opponents frequently talk more about his *mental* toughness than his *physical* skills. Michael, they say, can beat you through his sheer force of will. Wouldn't it be great to have people say the same thing about you?

Now, if Jordan had viewed his life only in terms of whether or not he made it as a professional baseball player, he would have been a failure. But as a wise, optimistic, and self-motivated person, Jordan understood that life is a process, and that failure can be a part of it. One thing Jordan did not fear, obviously, was criticism from others. But many people *are* paralyzed by a fear of being criticized. *What will people say? What will they think about me? How can I handle their criticism?*

If you wait around for everyone you know to approve everything you do, you'll still be waiting when the lights go out for the last time. This is called *paralysis by analysis*. If those closest to you are critical of a risk you plan to take, listen to them, weigh their advice for what it is worth, and then do what you think is best based on your evaluation of all aspects of your life. Just as it is important to view failure as a step in the process of success, it is important also to handle criticism in a constructive manner.

Let's say your boss comes up to you at the end of the workweek and hands you this criticism to take home for the weekend: *Your work this week was not up to par. I'm afraid you've been coasting in the job, and I want to see you put more effort into it or we're going to have to make a change in your assignment.*

Ouch. That sort of criticism, while certainly not mean-spirited, can make for a long ride home on a Friday night. Or maybe not. Maybe, just maybe, it could *energize* you to push yourself to the outer limits of your abilities, making your boss happy, and perhaps expanding your potential for bettering your life.

Here are three very different responses that you could have to the criticism delivered by your boss. Which one of them is the healthiest and most beneficial?

## 1. *I'm worthless and I'm weak.*

The boss's words weigh on you like a waterbed mattress dumped on your back, getting heavier and heavier as the negative thoughts flow in. *I'm in over my head. I can't do this job. I am a screw-up.* Overwhelmed by negative thoughts, you sink into depression and spend the weekend lying on the couch, feeling sorry for yourself, and drinking Maalox by the glass because you can't handle the thought of returning to work on Monday. When you do drag yourself back into the office, the boss sees immediately that you have not taken his words to heart and he puts you on probation. Your response is self-defeating and rooted in a negative approach to life. Criticism is viewed as the end result, the killing blow.

## 2. *The boss has never liked me. I don't like how he treats me.*

As soon as the boss walks away, you throw your entire supply of paper clips across the room and stomp out. On the way home, your knuckles turn white from your death grip on the poor steering wheel. You pull into the driveway, run over a tricycle, get out and kick the cat over the neighbor's fence. Anger—seething, boiling, red-faced anger—has you in its hold. You spend the weekend building yourself into a full rage, charge into work on Monday morning like an ugly storm, and let the boss have it. He responds by handing you your termination notice and pointing the way to the unemployment office. You have taken his criticism as a personal affront, and it has poisoned your judgment.

## 3. *What can I do to get back on track?*

Instead of taking the criticism as a knife to the heart or as a personal insult, you take it as an opportunity to *review and improve* your performance. Is there validity in what the boss said? How does my performance compare to that of my co-workers? What are they doing that I am not doing? What can I do to show the boss that I am committed to improving? You go home in a contemplative mood, sobered by the criticism, but not defeated by it. You spend the weekend doing constructive things, while also weighing the best approach to the workweek ahead. You go in on Monday, tell the boss that you have taken his criticism to heart and that you are going to rededicate yourself to your work. You have used criticism as a building block.

Think about the way you have handled criticism in the past. Which category of response matches your response? How might you have handled criticism in a more constructive manner?

I was criticized for: _____

My response to the criticism was: _____

_____

The result of my response was: _____

_____

Outside the workplace, criticism takes on a different dimension. Many people fear it because they place so much emphasis on being accepted. We all want to be liked. We all want to please other people. The problem is maintaining a balance between controlling our own lives and winning the acceptance and approval of the people we care about. This is a dilemma that confronts many people for the first time in their teen years. For teenagers in particular, it is very important to fit in and be accepted by their peers, and as a result, this is a point in life when many people first come to that fork in the road where they have to decide whether to do what they think is right for themselves, or to do what will win the approval of those around them.

I wish they taught classes in this in junior high to prepare people. It takes so much courage to face criticism or even rejection from your peers, and it is so hard to hang on to your own conscience and good judgment when others are pressuring to go along to get along. I was recently reminded of this when news accounts surfaced of a group of teenagers in Florida who went on a criminal rampage that began with just some vandalism but eventually resulted in them murdering a high school band instructor. These teens apparently had even considered going to Disney World and killing people there. In the early reports, it was written that the teens in the group were mostly very good students who had given up their own good judgment to follow a classmate who had become their leader.

It's a frightening thing, and not uncommon, for one person with bad intentions to corrupt others into following him. Often, it begins when someone is afraid to face criticism from a friend or acquaintance and classmate. You have to have faith in your own judgment and in your own value as a person in these circumstances.

I have a friend who was ostracized from the in crowd in high school because he refused to go along with things that they were doing. He took a lot of heat over it, but a few years later a girl he had gone to school with wrote to him and told him how much she had come to admire him for standing up for what he thought was right. Needless to say, my friend has done well in this world because of his faith in his own judgment, and his ability to take a stand when necessary. On the other hand, those young people in Florida have done things that they and their loved ones will have to pay for, probably for the rest of their lives.

It is also true in relationships that some people are so eager to please and to be loved that they give away too much of themselves. They let the other person dominate them, even hurt them physically, because they are so eager to have a relationship and to feel loved. It is often difficult to find the middle road in these situations, particularly for teenagers and especially for someone who has not been grounded in a loving and secure family life at home.

But it is vital to protect yourself in these situations so that you are not taken advantage of. Every person has value. Every person deserves to be respected. No one has the right to abuse you mentally or physically. Here are some helpful guidelines to assist you.

## TRYING TOO HARD

You should consider whether you are giving up too much to please others and to avoid criticism *if*:

- You are trying to get people to like you rather than respect you.
- You do things you know are wrong simply to gain approval.
- You do something you really don't want to do for someone who doesn't really have your best interests at heart.
- It seems like you can't do enough to please someone.
- A friendship or relationship seems like more work than fun.

Believe me, it is worth the risk to face criticism and rejection if it means keeping your self-respect. Now, that doesn't mean that you shouldn't care about how other people feel about you, but you can't allow other people to dictate to you how you live your life, particularly if they have not established that they have your best interests at heart. Here are a few things to strive for so that you can handle criticism and risk disapproval while pursuing your vision for a better life.

### RISKY BUSINESS: RULES FOR PLEASING YOURSELF FIRST

*Risk One: Take pleasure in being in control of your own life.*

Unless you enjoy wearing a sign on your back that says, "Kick me," you should take pleasure in running your own life. Don't cater to the whims of others. You should be thoughtful of other people and their needs, but only because you want to, not because they demand it. You give up too much of yourself when you forfeit control of your life to others by catering to their demands or trying to live up to their expectations rather than your own.

### Risk Two: Feel free to express your uniqueness and your own needs.

There seems to be so much pressure today to fit in with the crowd, to be just one more store in the franchise rather than a one-of-a-kind creation. I encourage you to express your own talents and gifts and to celebrate them without feeling pressure to wear the same clothes, do the same things, and to follow the crowd even if you don't care to. If blending in makes you feel more comfortable, fine, but don't feel like you have to submerge your own personality to win approval.

### Risk Three: Do not feel guilty about saying no.

This one isn't in the Ten Commandments nor is it in the U.S. Constitution, exactly, but it should be. You have the right to say no and the responsibility to say no if that is what you judge to be the proper response. You may not be correct. You may be the only one. It may make you unpopular. But it is your right. Have no fear, have no guilt, say no whenever and wherever you judge it to be in your best interest. They can argue with your judgment, but not with your right to make that judgment.

### Risk Four: Let them know where you stand, loudly and proudly.

Do not be afraid to take a stand, or to let people know that you have taken a stand. No one respects a wishy-washy person.

Don't force your opinions on other people. Don't expect others to applaud every time you offer an opinion. But feel free to exercise your free will, and to let others know that you are willing to take a stand even when it might not be popular.

*Risk Five: Be curious about life and all that it has to offer you.*

Too often, we pull back from things that interest us for fear that we will be criticized by other people. *Classical music? That's for nerds. You're working with the handicapped? What are you, a do-gooder?* Some of the things I enjoy the most now are things that initially I was afraid to risk trying simply because I didn't want to appear inept or to face criticism. Feel free to check out the things that interest *you*. If someone else doesn't like it, that's too bad.

## YOUR RISK-TAKING PROFILE

Are you a risk-taker? Answer the following questions to determine your willingness to take risks.

1. What is the one risk you could take today that would move you most efficiently and effectively toward fulfilling your vision of a better life?

_____

_____

2. What is the one thing you fear the most about taking that risk?

_____

_____

3. What one habit holds you back from taking that risk?

_____

_____

4. How would taking this risk change your life?

_____

_____

## RISK MANAGEMENT

Thinking about your willingness to take risks helps you focus on what you need to do to get on track to pursue your goals. You have to be prepared to take risks and to try new approaches in order to keep moving along in the Success Process. A key lesson here is that *if you continue to do what you have always done, you will continue to get the same result you have always gotten. But if you take well-calculated risks by changing your approach, you can make great progress.* There are people who never have to take risks. Whether born to wealth or handed it, they find success without having to test themselves by taking chances. But most of us are not so fortunate. Most of us have to take risks to pursue our vision for a better life. We have to go out there into the outer limits, where we may not have as much control of our lives. We have to overcome our fears and live *courageously.*

Risk is like a coin with two sides. On one there is the possibility of failure, on the other is the opportunity for gain. You must always carefully measure whether a risk is worth taking, and that means considering the fact that sometimes *doing nothing about your situation is itself a risk.*

Some people think they can avoid risk by staying with the familiar, but as tens of thousands of people in the workplace have learned in recent years, there is no longer any such thing as a risk-free life. It used to be thought that if you could get hired by IBM or AT&T or nearly any other Fortune 500 corporation, you could rely on being employed there until it was time for the gold watch, a fat pension, and the retirement condo in Florida. But from 1979 to 1996, the Fortune 500 companies, which have generally been the most stable and best-paying in this country, cut their workforces by a total of more than 5 million people.

Brian Barnes's job was one of fifty thousand cut by Sears in Chicago in the early 1990s. He was fifty-three years old and had worked for "Mother Sears" for twenty-nine years. "What our generation did was we placed our careers in the hands of our employer," he told the *Chicago Tribune*. "There was a social compact that corporate America had with its people. We no longer have that."

Now, we know that there are no guarantees in the job market, and in truth, there is no such thing as a risk-free environment in any aspect of life. It is important to also note that often there is as much risk in doing nothing as there is in taking a risk that enables you to pursue your vision of a better life.

## CALCULATING RISKS

Your ability to take risks successfully depends largely on your decision-making skills and also in your approach to risk-taking. First of all, you have to understand what deeply held needs, desires, and values motivate your behavior. If you aren't certain of your goals and clear in your vision for your life, then you are ill-prepared to take risks that will move you toward that goal.

Before taking risks, then, you again have to go back and check your vision, by evaluating whether the risk you are considering is in line with the principles that you have chosen to guide your life. Are you considering taking the risk for a good reason, or for ego? Is the risk appealing to you because it will help you lead a better, more worthwhile, and challenging life, or will it simply mean more money, more prestige, or more physical gratification?

There is something important to consider here: *If you take a risk for the wrong reasons, you may be sabotaging yourself.* And so it is best to measure that risk against your principles, values, and beliefs before you make the leap. Here are a few questions to ask yourself:

1. What lies on the other side? If you take this risk, where will it put you in the Success Process?

_____

_____

_____

2. Will it add to the strength of your support foundation, which consists of your relationships, your career, your community? Or will it weaken any aspect of that foundation?

_____

_____

_____

3. What is the allure of this risk? Why does it appeal to you?

_____

_____

_____

4. Write down the potential benefits of the risk:

_____

_____

5. Write down the potential problems (downside) of the risk:

_____

_____

6. Now weigh the potential benefits against the downside and ask yourself, *Will this move me closer to fulfilling my vision for my life, or could it potentially set me back?*

_____

_____

## LOOK BEFORE YOU LEAP

Taking a risk is like physically leaping over an obstacle or a chasm that separates you from what you want. If you are certain that the object on the other side is what you want, you can make that leap with determination, enthusiasm, and fully focused. But if you aren't so sure, you won't be as determined, enthusiastic, and focused, and in all likelihood you won't make it. Instead of taking opportunities as they appear, you will be torn by indecision and ambivalence. And that is the most precarious position you can possibly be in. In every wildlife documentary I've ever seen, the predator always gets the one animal that can't decide which way to run.

Now, we aren't impalas running from the lions, so we can take time to carefully evaluate the risks we take so that we can take them with a certain amount of confidence. One thing that is necessary, though, is to overcome any doubts and fears you might have. You cannot live your life out of fear of what might happen. You must live out of your vision for a better life. The greatest reason people do not take risks is fear of the unknown.

We all have fears. In fact, some studies have found more than a hundred secret fears held by people, everything ranging from fear of open spaces to fear of closed spaces, fear of heights and fear of depths. We're afraid of spiders, snakes, and mosquitoes. Fear is a learned response. We are not born with it; that is why parents have to watch their young children so closely. Fears that are learned can be unlearned. A child who fears dogs because a mean dog chased her can learn to like dogs if exposed to friendly ones. Fears are real only when we make them real by investing too much into them. When we allow fear to dominate our lives, we give it too much power. Some people allow their fears to affect their health. It's been said that fears kill more people than work because some people spend more time in fear than they do in working.

The only real cure for fear is faith and courage. You have to have faith that there really is no bogeyman under the bed, and the courage to look down there and confirm it. Fears can haunt and control us when we lack faith in our ability to overcome them and the courage to take them on. Fear defeats us when we allow it to condition our minds, to make us cowards. Have you ever been forced by an emergency to do something you were afraid to do, something you never thought you could do? Have you ever leaped higher or run faster than you ever thought you could because you knew *you had to do it*? That is the form of energy you need to tap into to overcome your fear of taking risks. You have to develop a sort of *crisis mentality* to summon the courage to overcome such fears. You have to decide that taking this risk is vital to your life.

One method for gaining the faith and confidence necessary to take on your fears is to purposely confront them. Name a fear that you have and then come up with a way to confront and overcome it. If you have a fear of heights, you might go to the roof of a tall building and make yourself stand there to overcome that fear. If you are afraid of flying, plan a long flight on a big airliner. Do these things as if your life depended on them.

The fear that is holding me back from pursuing a better life is:

_____

_____

To overcome it, I will:

_____

_____

## THE SLIDE FOR LIFE

Often, fear is the only thing that stands between us and our vision for a better life, and if you don't develop the courage to overcome those fears, you might never have the opportunity to reach your dreams and goals. There was a boy who grew up in the South Bronx to immigrant Jamaican parents. He was not a particularly good student; he was a mediocre athlete, and not overly ambitious as a young man. He seemed to find himself, though, when he joined the ROTC in high school. He discovered leadership abilities that he didn't know he possessed. And so, he set his sights on a military career.

But then early in his basic training, he met a challenge that forced him to overcome a fear or give up on his dream. It was called, dramatically enough, "The Slide for Life." It was a cable strung a hundred feet above a river, between two trees. It started high in one tree, and dropped steeply to the tree on the other side of the river. The young soldier had to ride down that cable on a hook attached to a pulley that ran along it. He was not allowed to let go, falling safely into the river, until the instructor issued the command—at the very last second before he would crash into the tree.

It was "the moment I had my first doubt about the career I had chosen," Colin Powell later wrote in his autobiography, *My American Journey.* "It was one of the most frightening experiences of my life."

But he did it. He overcame his doubts and fears and took the risk because he knew it was a necessary step in his pursuit of a career in the military. Had he chickened out or refused to face his fears, it is doubtful that Colin Powell would have succeeded in the military. His same willingness to take risks later resulted in Powell's applying for a White House fellowship, which propelled him to even higher levels as the National Security Adviser to the President of the United States and, eventually, Chairman of the Joint Chiefs of Staff.

Colin Powell realizes that there is no progress without struggle. You will never get to the next level if you don't widen your experience and base of knowledge, and often that involves taking risks.

Remember these rules for taking risks:

- The most important risks to take are those that will move you most quickly toward your goals.
- Failure to take risks limits your opportunities and new experiences.
- By avoiding risks, you are giving in to fears and missing opportunities.
- Failure can provide an opportunity to learn. Some of the most useful lessons are learned as a result of things that didn't work out.

- In order to evaluate a risk, you have to keep focused on your own needs, desires, and values.
- Fear can be managed when you have faith in your ability to solve problems that might result.
- If you focus on your fears rather than on your goals, you miss opportunities and fail to achieve your vision.

# Chapter 7
# Pilot the Seasons of Change

>>>>>>>>>>>>>>>>>>>>>>>>>

*How most of us dread change, fight against it, or, refuse to acknowledge it, even unto the last look in the coffin.*

GWENDOLYN BROOKS

A FRIEND OF MINE, Daniel, was forced to change departments within the corporation he works for. He and nearly all of his co-workers were moved to new areas because of a change in the mission of their division. Many of them had worked in that division for years in jobs that were coveted by others in the company.

Most of Daniel's co-workers reacted emotionally to being transferred. Anger and despair were the most common responses. There were many heated meetings with supervisors and department heads. Several people threatened to quit and a few came close to being fired because of their vocal opposition to the changes being made. Although it is normal to experience emotional reactions to change, often people get so caught up in those emotions that they lose their way temporarily, and make poor decisions that can have a lasting impact.

Learning how to manage your response to change is crucial if you are going to pursue the Success Process. We are at the point in the journey through the Success Process in which changes are to be expected and dealt with in a constructive manner. Change is an integral part of the process, and I know that many people have difficulty in dealing with change, even those changes that they may anticipate. Yet change is essential if you are to better your life. After all, if you are satisfied with the way things are, why do you want a better life? You must change the way you have been living if you want to change the results you have been getting.

## SUMMONING THE POWER TO CHANGE

So far in this book, we have looked at how to:

- Increase your self-awareness so that you are in control of emotions and feelings that may have held you back in the past.
- Create a vision of your dreams and goals.
- Develop a plan to pursue those goals.
- Come up with your own Rules of the Road to stay focused on your plan without losing sight of the people and principles that are important to you.
- Take the risks necessary to move forward.

The purpose of each of those steps is to bring about a change in your life, a change for the better. But even minor changes in your life can trigger strong feelings. A change in your daily routine such as the failure of your morning newspaper to arrive or a delay on your commuter train can throw you off for a good part of the day. Bigger changes evoke even stronger emotions and feelings. A death in the family, the sudden loss of a job, an automobile accident: these unexpected events carry with them intense feelings that may interfere with our ability to function.

Even outwardly positive changes, such as a move to a nicer house, can bring with it intense feelings of sadness and disorientation, brought on by leaving what had been a more familiar and comfortable environment—a settled house, friendly neighbors, and known surroundings such as schools, stores, and traffic routes. Even though the new house might have been a goal, the satisfaction of moving in can be soured by such feelings, particularly if they are unanticipated. Such unexpected feelings can tend to make us resent even positive change, unless we learn to deal with them. That is what *managing your response to change* is all about.

Fourteen-year-old Phanedra Harper was extremely nervous about a change her mother forced her to undergo a few years ago. The Chicago teenager, who lives in a public housing project, was not doing well in her crowded public school, where teachers were forced to deal with so many distractions, including the threat of gang violence, that it was impossible for them to give additional attention, particularly to a fairly capable student such as Phanedra. But her mother dreamed that her daughter would make it to college and find a better life, so she brought about a change; she enrolled Phanedra in an after-school program at the Metro Achievement Center, a federally sponsored educational facility designed to help inner-city girls get into Chicago's best high schools.

Phanedra was so nervous about making the change that when she first entered the Metro program, she was afraid to speak. But within a few months, she was not only speaking freely, she was pulling As and Bs instead of Bs and Cs. Phanedra's willingness to manage her reaction to change and to work through her nervousness resulted in her getting into one of Chicago's best high schools. "At Metro, I had individual tutoring that helped my self-confidence," she told a newspaper reporter.

A key point in this chapter is that *just as change is natural, so are the feelings that accompany it*. Daniel felt considerable sadness in leaving his old department. He had loved his job there. He had often commented that it was the best job he had ever had. But he understood that his feelings of sadness were natural, so he did not resent or fight the change that caused them. He accepted his feelings without letting them affect his behavior. He effectively managed a change in his life and, as a result, he has been praised by his supervisors for making the transition smoothly from his former department to a new one. *"Change is part of my job just as it is part of life,"* he told me. *"It is silly to be afraid of change or to fight it, because, before you know it, there will be another change coming behind it."*

Think about a recent change in your life, whether it was a move to a new home, a change in your job, a change in a personal relationship.

Write down the change that occurred: _____

_____

Note how you felt about the change.

The positive emotions I experienced with the change were:

_____

The negative emotions I experienced with the change were:

_____

Were you surprised by those emotions? Overall, do you now regard the change as a positive, or as a negative experience? Do any of the fears, concerns, or negative emotions that you experienced now seem validated, or invalid?

Do you think you could have managed your response to the change better?

## CONTROLLING YOUR ANGER

Controlling the anger that sometimes is triggered by unexpected or unwelcome change is extremely important. The anger is, in truth, fleeting, but the effects of that anger can be long-lasting and highly damaging to your pursuit of a better life.

Daniel became extremely concerned over one co-worker in particular. This guy became so embittered that he was openly hostile and rebellious toward their supervisors. Considered a valuable employee, he nonetheless could not control his bitterness, and he became self-destructive in his work habits and attitudes. His career took a steep dive that he has yet to recover from.

FIVE TIPS FOR CONTROLLING YOUR ANGER IN TIMES
OF CHANGE

### 1. Step back and look at the big picture.

Anger is a natural response. In times of danger or stress, anger triggers increased blood flow and the adrenaline that prepared ancient man for flight or fight. Nature created this emotion to serve a purpose, but you want to make sure it serves *your* purpose. Is your anger and resentment misdirected? Are you directing it at the real source of your resentment? And even if you have the right target, are you hurting yourself? Don't sabotage your own career or relationships because of fleeting anger. Put the anger aside and assess the situation thoughtfully, and if your anger is being vented in a self-destructive manner, find another way to vent it.

### 2. Remove yourself from the scene of the crime.

If a change in the workplace or in a relationship has triggered powerful feelings of anger and resentment, make a strategic retreat. Take that anger somewhere and let it vent on the racquet-ball court or a ten-mile jog. If it is a more lasting and pervasive anger, now is the time for a vacation or a sabbatical to a remote mountain cabin or an isolated beach. Do yourself, and those around you, a favor, in order to avoid lasting damage.

### 3. Transform negative emotions to positive action.

If you are angry with an employer, use that energy to write résumés and test the job market. If the anger is directed at someone close to you, use the energy to widen your circle of friends. Don't do anything to be hurtful or vengeful; do something positive to ease your anger and to gain perspective.

### 4. Talk it out.

Gather friends or sympathetic co-workers who are not immediately involved in whatever is triggering your anger; go somewhere away from the scene of the crime, and talk through your anger to avoid saying or doing things that will only hurt you or your cause.

### 5. Take stock of your options.

Many times anger is the result of feeling trapped and robbed of opportunities, but in truth your anger may be blinding you to the opportunities that await. It has been said that in times of change, people concentrate far too much on the door that has been closed, rather than looking for those that have been opened. Rather than being swept up emotionally, charge up mentally and consider what opportunities might have opened up by the change that has triggered your anger. Now is the time to act, not react.

## CHANGING FOR THE GOOD

Daniel was not one of those who put up a fight. He had enjoyed his job immensely, but he knew that in his line of work, nothing was permanent. He felt that change was part of the job, and so when it came, he accepted it. His new job was not as satisfying personally, but it is a higher-profile position valued by the corporation's top echelon.

Although he had his concerns about the change, Daniel is doing very well in the new job. And, somewhat surprisingly, so are most of those who resented and fought the change. As it turned out, their old department was completely revamped, and because of poor planning and bad management, it has deteriorated from being a highly desirable place to work to one that is regarded as a problem area for the company. Those who left the department are now glad to no longer be there. Those who were allowed to remain wish that they had been transferred as well. They too have discovered that often it is better to *manage how you respond to change* and profit from it than to resist it and be left behind.

Few people would disagree with that. Why then do so many treat any and every proposed change as if it were a deadly disease? That attitude is so entrenched, particularly in many work environments, that a popular office poster is entitled *Fifty Reasons Why We/It/They Can't Change*. And these are the reasons given:

1. We've never done it before.
2. Nobody else has ever done it.
3. It has never been tried before.
4. We tried it before.
5. Another company/person tried it before.
6. We've been doing it this way for 25 years.

7. It doesn't work in a small company.
8. It won't work in a large company.
9. It won't work in our company.
10. Why change—it's working OK.
11. The boss will never buy it.
12. It needs further investigation.
13. Our competitors are not doing it.
14. It's too much trouble to change.
15. Our company is different.
16. The ad department says it can't be sold.
17. Production says it's a bad idea.
18. The service department won't like it.
19. The janitor says it can't be done.
20. It can't be done.
21. We don't have the money.
22. We don't have the personnel.
23. We don't have the equipment.
24. The union will scream.
25. It's too visionary.
26. You can't teach an old dog new tricks.
27. It's too radical a change.
28. It's beyond my responsibility.
29. It's not my job.
30. We don't have the time.
31. It will make other procedures obsolete.
32. Customers won't buy it.
33. It's contrary to policy.
34. It will increase overhead.
35. The employees will never buy it.
36. It's not our problem.
37. I don't like it.
38. You're right but . . .
39. We're not ready for it.
40. It needs more thought.

41. Management won't accept it.
42. We can't take the chance.
43. We'd lose money on it.
44. It takes too long to pay out.
45. We're doing all right as it is.
46. It needs committee study.
47. Competition won't like it.
48. It needs sleeping on.
49. It won't work in this department.
50. It's impossible.

Do any of those reasons for not making a change sound familiar? Resistance to change is nearly as certain, and as inevitable, as change itself. Our society is always boiling with change: changing fashions, changing technology, changing mores, changing markets. It seems that change occurs more rapidly with each passing year. Such constant change is like an unrelenting and powerful wind or water current that can wear down trees and even rock.

## TWO TYPES OF CHANGE

There are two types of changes: those that are more or less forced upon you by changing circumstances, and those that you bring about yourself in order to create opportunities. Daniel and his co-workers were forced to deal with the changes brought on by their employer. That sort of change can be difficult to deal with, but it is perhaps even more difficult to deal with change that you have created in your life.

Dealing well with changing circumstances is important, but *creating and managing* your response to change in your life is probably an even greater part of the Success Process. If you are to seek a better life than the one you have now, you have to make your own changes. That takes courage, and dealing with change, even positive change, requires even more self-control, patience, and perseverance. Change can overwhelm people emotionally, so that their power to reason is diminished and their vision of a better life is obscured.

When you think about it, we really have no choice about managing our response to change if we are going to live the Success Process. If we are going to constantly seek better lives, we have to change. We have to change from just going along and getting along to chasing our dreams and challenging life. Change is the catalyst for action in our lives. It is what ignites the spark into a flame; it transforms the drop of water into a torrent.

To enact change, we have to let go of where we have been in order to move on to where we want to go. I see this acted out sometimes when I look out the kitchen window to the playground a few blocks away. From the high-rise building in Chicago where I live, I can see parents helping their children get started on a set of monkey bars on the playground. Young children often have trouble with these monkey bars. Their parents will lift them up to the first rung, but youngsters often are afraid to let go with one hand to grab the next bar so they can go across the full length of the bars.

Quite naturally, they are afraid that if they let go with one hand, they won't be able to hold on long enough to reach the next bar. But once they get the hang of it, they understand that in order to move across the bars, they have to follow a process of holding on with one hand, letting go with the other, getting a grip on the next bar, and pulling themselves forward.

The children are naturally fearful of changing their positions by letting go of one bar in order to grab the one ahead. At first they don't understand or have faith in the process involved. When they come to understand it, though, they willingly make the changes necessary to move ahead. The Success Process works much the same way. Often, you can't move ahead or make a change in life without letting go of what you have. If you want a better job, you have to leave the old one. If your relationship isn't working, you have to end it and move on. If your current circumstances are not satisfactory, you have to leave them to get the results you want. As Albert Einstein said, "The significant problems we face cannot be solved at the same level of thinking we were at when we created them." We can't always find the answers within our existing environment; sometimes we have to enact change in order to find answers.

We all have to learn to welcome, accept, and even bring about change as a natural part of the process of bettering out lives. To do that, you have to *be resilient*. You can't insist on doing what you've always done, otherwise you'll just keep getting what you have always gotten. And you have to be patient with the process of change, understanding that it will be accompanied by periods of sadness, disorientation, and even a lack of apparent progress as you adjust to your new circumstances.

Write down something that you want to change in order to better your life; for example, your level of education, your degree of fitness, your marital status, or your circle of friends.

The change I would like to make is: _____

_____

What has stopped you from making this change in the past?

_____

_____

_____

What fears and emotions can you anticipate when making this change?

_____

_____

_____

What criticisms from within and from others will accompany this change?

_____

_____

_____

How will making this change make your life better?

_____

_____

_____

What other changes, good and bad, will accompany this one?

Good changes: _____

Bad changes: _____

Will it be worthwhile to make this change in your life?

_____

What steps do you have to go through to bring about this change?

_____

_____

_____

## VIEWING THE PROCESS OF CHANGE

I had you do that exercise to get you thinking about *the process of change.* This process generally involves some common and identifiable stages. Each stage is accompanied by certain emotions and feelings. In describing another process common to human experience, the grieving process, psychiatrists say that we can come to terms with loss such as the death of a loved one or the breakup of a relationship only by allowing ourselves to go through the full range of emotions. When you deny yourself the expression of these emotions, you run the risk of delaying your emotional responses over years and years, extending the grieving process. It is not unusual for one or more family members to experience this with a death in the family. These individuals may not mourn as openly at the funeral, but then days or even months later they break down for no apparent reason, in what is known as *delayed grief.*

The lesson to be drawn from examining the grieving process is that *you cannot cheat your feelings.* You may be able to suppress them for a while, but eventually, in one form or another, they will express themselves. And so, in the process of change, it is far better to recognize, understand, and accept your emotional responses while not allowing them to influence important, long-range decisions.

Often, people facing a change in their lives try to cheat their feelings by playing down their feelings of loss and sadness, but as in the instance of delayed grief, those emotions will eventually come to the forefront. It is important, then, to understand and accept that when you make changes, you will probably have to let go of some aspect of your life. Acknowledge that ending, deal with it in your own way, and then go on to the new beginning brought on by change.

## NAVIGATING THE SEASONS OF CHANGE

Sometimes, people react to change in their life as though it is a rare and shocking experience. But our entire lives are a cycle of constant change, seasons of change, as reflected in this beautiful and familiar psalm from Ecclesiastes:

> *To every thing there is a season, and a time to every purpose under heaven:*
> *A time to be born, and a time to die; a time to plant, and a time to pluck up that which is planted;*
> *A time to kill, and a time to heal; a time to break down, and a time to build up;*
> *A time to weep, and a time to laugh; a time to mourn, and a time to dance;*
> *A time to cast away stones, and a time to gather stones together; a time to embrace, and a time to refrain from embracing;*
> *A time to get, and a time to lose; a time to keep, and a time to cast away;*
> *A time to rend, and a time to sew; a time to keep silence, and a time to speak;*
> *A time to love, and a time to hate; a time of war, and a time of peace.*

The first stage in learning to master change is accepting that change is not an *event*, it is a *natural process*, like the change of seasons in nature. Each change in seasons occurs in a predictable sequence and each involves stages that must be completed in order to move to the next level of transition. The process of change is similar. Changes in your life are often accompanied by emotional responses that range from a sense of loss and sadness to a feeling of disorientation and lethargy, and then gradual rejuvenation and exhilaration. These emotions mirror, in many ways, the moods and emotions that accompany the changing seasons in nature.

## STAGE ONE: LETTING GO

Nature provides a great model for the process of mastering change in our lives. Fall is probably the season that we most associate with change because of its spectacular display in the changing colors of leaves. And so, to help you understand and master the process of change, let's start with fall, the season of change in which we *let go*.

Fall, or autumn, is a season of paradox. It marks the beginning of the school year, of the football season, and, in the colder climates, sweater weather. Yet it is also a season that marks the end of summer, the end of school vacation, the end of the growing season. Fall, then, is a season ripe with change. What feelings and emotions do you associate with the season of fall? Note them below:

_____

_____

_____

Look back at the emotions and feelings that you wrote down in association with the season of fall. If you are like most people, you have mixed emotions about this season. It is an invigorating time in many respects, with the crispness in the air that brings red to your cheeks. But it is also the time in which you say goodbye to the joys of summer, the warm days outdoors, swimming, sunbathing, working in the garden, and basking in the outdoors.

The emotions and feelings associated with fall are very similar to those commonly experienced in the letting-go stage of change in our lives. There is a certain excitement and rejuvenation at the changes coming, but also a melancholy over acknowledging that the period also marks an ending. Many times, this is the stage of change that people have the hardest time handling. As many of

Daniel's co-workers exhibited, it is not easy to let go of what has been comfortable and familiar.

Just as the trees cut off nourishment to their leaves in the fall, the process of change begins with the act of letting go that part of life we want to change. If the trees didn't release their old leaves, their branches would not be able to sprout buds for new growth. The same is true for you and me. Our personal growth can come only when we let go of old ways and self-defeating behavior that has held us back from bettering our lives.

In any change, something is lost, whether planned or unplanned. That is a fact that many people have difficulty dealing with when faced with change. As much as they may want to change their lives, they don't want to let go of what they have. It's like the child on the monkey bars who wants to go across, but is afraid to change the position of his hands to do it.

In the process of change in your life, it is natural to feel regrets and sadness and some fear over letting go of what has been familiar, even if it hasn't always been pleasant, even if you want to change it. So you shouldn't let those feelings stop you from going through with changes that can open the possibilities to a better life. When I left Bob Brown's public relations firm to strike out on my own, I was full of fear over making the move. I really knew nothing about running my own business. I had enjoyed working with him. But I wanted to make a leap in my pursuit of a dream to have my own business in Chicago, and so I accepted my fears and concerns as a natural part of the process of change, and then I went ahead. Oftentimes you don't know how to get where you want to go, but the most debilitating thing you can do is to let that stymie you. You won't find your way out of a maze by standing still or looking back, but if you move about, it is more likely that the way will reveal itself.

When the people in Daniel's office reacted to their fears and sadness at changes in the workplace, they weren't wrong in recognizing their emotions, but they were too focused on what

PILOT THE SEASONS OF CHANGE

they were leaving. They would have been better off focusing on what was ahead of them. The truth was, as soon as their company decided to change the mission of their department, that aspect of their lives was over. It would never be the same place. They would never feel the same way about it. And so, they should have recognized that change was inevitable and made the best of it. To respond any other way was self-defeating.

Here are a few suggestions on what you can do to help yourself let go of the past in order to make positive changes within your Success Circles governing your relationships, your job or career, and your place in the community.

• Be attuned to your emotions during this stage of the change process. Monitor your feelings and your attitudes toward those around you. It is important to practice self-awareness during this stage, so that you don't allow your emotions to cloud your judgment or to spark negative behavior.

• Recognize that feelings of sadness and anger are naturally associated with the sense of loss that change initially brings. There is no need to fight these feelings. That only brings more turmoil. Take the sadness or anger and channel it into positive energy by accepting it, understanding why you feel the way you do. If you are sad, do something that makes you laugh or elevates your mood. If you are angry, use that energy to do something constructive that you've been putting off, such as exercising or working around the house.

• Acknowledge the validity of the feelings and the importance of the loss. Put your moods into perspective and grant yourself permission to respond appropriately. There is no reason to feel guilty or angry at yourself for responding to perfectly valid emotions.

• Say goodbye in your own way to the people, places, and things that will be left behind. It is vital to reach closure emotionally—to accept what has happened, validate the emotions that have arisen, and acknowledge the change that has resulted.

## STAGE TWO: THE WINTER DOLDRUMS

The letting go period of enacting change is followed by a stage that compares to winter, a season of the doldrums, marked by inactivity, stagnation, or a productivity slump. After we let go of our past circumstances in making a decision to change our lives, it is common to feel these doldrums, a lingering sadness and a loss of direction. But, as in wintertime, this also is a period for refortifying strength, a time in which we can reflect on our lives and get in touch with our needs, values, and desires in preparation for a new beginning.

Write down the emotions and feelings that the winter season brings to mind for you:

_____

_____

_____

In many ways, winter is a time for reflection, so it sparks images of thoughtfulness and contemplation. It is a period when families gather to celebrate the holiday season and the end of one year and the beginning of another. Winter is marked by a hiatus in nature. Most trees and plants appear lifeless, though they are not. They are simply pausing to gather strength for the next season.

When making a change in your life, there may come a point when you feel as though you have made a mistake in giving up the old and chancing something new. This too is a natural reaction at this stage of the change process. Rosabeth Moss Kanter, author of *The Change Masters*, was referring to it when she wrote that "every change looks like failure in the middle."

It is natural to feel anxious when making a change. Think again of those children on the climbing bars and how anxious they are in that split second before they have to let go of one bar in order to reach for the next. Understand and acknowledge your anxiety at this stage but don't despair. Stick with your plans to pursue a better life. You may want to give up, or go back to the old way, but you have to be courageous when you are chasing a dream.

Give yourself credit for having put enough thought into your decision to change *before* you took the action. This is no time for second thoughts or looking over your shoulder. This is the period for hunkering down and going ahead, for having faith in yourself and your decision to change. Not to frighten you, but it could be disastrous to turn back on your decision at this point, because you have already altered your old situation by leaving it. The way things were no longer exists. It is better to follow through and to look ahead to the better life that you have planned for yourself.

Instead of despairing or giving up, you should use this time to sort out feelings, and reflect on your needs, values, and desires while gathering strength and resolve for the new beginning about to come. Here are a few suggestions to help you more effectively manage this period in the change process:

• Think of this as your period of hibernation. Take this time to recharge your energy levels, building up strength to face the changes that will bring you closer to the life you want for yourself and your loved ones. This is a good time to read motivational and inspirational books and also the biographies and writings of successful people, particularly those who have had experiences that you can relate to. Listen to inspirational and motivational tapes in your car; I do this all the time when driving and on airline flights. It makes good use of what would otherwise be wasted time. Also, this is a good period to arrange dinners and lunches with people who stoke your confidence and inspire you to strive and improve yourself. Get together with dynamic people who are taking life on.

• To help your concentration and focus, you might want to keep a journal in which you record your thoughts on where you have been in your life and where you want to go. Keeping a journal helps you express thoughts and feelings that you might not be conscious of otherwise. You don't have to record every thought. Just a page a day is a good start, although as you progress you may find yourself writing more and more.

• This is a good period also for huddling with your friends, loved ones, mentors, and role models and discussing with them the changes that you need to make in order to get what you want out of life. You don't have to ask their advice—they may not even agree with what you are doing—but it is always helpful to talk things out in order to come to a more complete understanding of your own feelings toward what is going on in your life.

## STAGE THREE: SPRING BLOSSOMS

While my friend Daniel spent very little time fretting over the change in his position, many of his co-workers went through an extended period of anger and sadness. But after a few months, they began to feel more comfortable in their new departments, and a number of them eventually felt rejuvenated by the change. That often happens when you persevere and work your way through the difficult aspects of undergoing change. If you hang in there, often you come to a point when you adjust, and then take pride in successfully managing a change in your life.

This period compares to the spring season, when nature renews itself and rapid change takes place. Spring is a favorite season for many people because of the beauty it brings in nature.

Write down some of the emotions and feelings you associate
with spring:

_____

_____

_____


Spring inspires a sense of anticipation, of eagerness and high
energy. You want to lie in the grass and let the warming sun
recharge your batteries. Similarly, this blossoming period in the
change process can involve rejuvenation and accelerated growth
that may be both exciting and a bit frightening. You know the old
saying, *Be careful what you ask for, you might get it!* Sometimes
when you stretch your talents and abilities in order to make a
change, it can be scary. It's like moving to a nicer and more expensive home. At first it may seem too big and the house payments might cause you some sleepless nights, but eventually the
rooms fill up with furniture, you adjust to the higher payments,
and a new level of comfort is established.

As I write this book, I find myself in this "blossoming" period
in my business. I spent several years planning and preparing for
this change, in which I moved from a sports marketing business
to a more diverse business. Early on, I wondered often if it was
the right thing to do. It was scary and at times I was a little down
about whether it was going to work, but suddenly things began
to fall together rapidly. In recent months, I've established a business presence in New York as well as Chicago, and the opportunities seem to be coming from all directions. This change in my
approach to business has taken on a life of its own. It is exhilarating and challenging just to keep up with it all.

This is the time when your vision is put to the test. This is
when you find out whether you are really on track to your
dream. It is a time when everything seems accelerated, every

emotion accentuated. You feel more alive than ever before. I've even had several friends comment that I've become visibly more focused and confident in my business in recent months. I feel good that I've managed this change in my life, that all of the seeds that I planted are now bearing fruit. As wonderful as this period in my life is, it is one that requires thoughtful handling. Otherwise, you can get swept away by all of the rapid developments and lose focus or feel overwhelmed.

Here are some things you can do to help manage this phase of change:

• This is the time to stop planning and get into action. Things begin to happen now because you have done your homework and laid the groundwork; now is the time to go with the flow and take advantage of the opportunities that open up. It can be daunting when change begins to ignite all around you. After so many years of planning, I now find myself bombarded with opportunities and proposals. In the past, I had to pass on such matters because I didn't feel that I had the resources to act upon them; but now I do, and it can be dizzying. But this is when you want to act upon your dreams.

• Be prepared to expand your vision. In this period of opportunity, keep in mind that you may need to adjust your vision for a better life to fit the growth you are undergoing. You may need to set your sights even higher than before to accommodate that growth. You certainly don't want to stop one day and look back and say, "I missed that opportunity to move to an even higher level." At the very least, you want to be alert to the fact that as your opportunities grow, you need to grow too. For example, I had designed my new company to have a variety of marketing, public relations, and entrepreneurial functions, but during this period I am seeing the opportunity to provide an even greater range of products and services.

• Take it step by step. In this period of rapid growth, that may mean you'll be stepping along at a brisk pace, if not sprinting, but keep in mind earlier lessons on setting direction for your vision, so that you always stay on course.

• Stay focused on your primary goals. There will be many, many temptations and distractions at this point of the change process, so you need to remind yourself of what your ultimate goal is and keep that vision in your mind. That doesn't mean that you can't explore other opportunities, but always ask yourself: *Is that where I want to go with my life?*

• Take care of your life. In such an exhilarating time, it is easy to focus on the change process and neglect other aspects of your life. Remember that a balanced life includes maintaining a healthy situation in your relationships, your work, and your community. Force yourself to exercise and to take time to nurture the personal relationships that are important to you.

## STAGE FOUR: MATURE GROWTH

In nature, summer is the season when plants reach mature growth and the process of sustaining life is played out in the cycle of reproduction. This is the period in which plants mature and find their purpose in the world. Summer is the time when all of the planning and hard work is rewarded. Write down some of the emotions and thoughts that this season brings to mind:

_____

_____

_____

Summer is a highly sociable time of year, when we gather to make new connections and to bask in our accomplishments before building upon them. The same holds for this final stage in the process of change in your life. This is when your preparation and experience bear fruit and sprout the seeds that will guarantee long-term growth. As exciting as it is for me right now with all of the opportunities coming my way, I look forward to the final phase, when I'll be able to reap the rewards and move on to even greater levels of experience and personal growth.

During this period, the focus is on continued growth. I foresee using this time to reflect on the opportunities that have opened up for my business and to carefully evaluate them so that I can choose those that are most in line with my vision. This is an extremely important time, in which decisions need to be made carefully. Here are some things to guide you in this period of change:

• This is definitely a time to check your bearings. Are you in line with your deeply held needs, desires, and values? Or have you become distracted and lured off the path of your vision for a better life? What do you need to do to get on track and to stay there? Begin to think now of where you need to head on the next leg of your journey to a better life. Let the seeds of your plan emerge now so that over the next few seasons they can germinate.

• Write out the options that are available to you at this point. Note which ones provide the greatest opportunity for continued growth that is consistent with where you want to go in life. Cross off those that take you in tempting directions that are not in line with your principles, values, and general guidelines for living.

• Bring in your closest advisers and confidants. How do they evaluate the options that are open for you? What do they think suits you best? Are they with you, or do they think you have strayed off the path that is best for you?

## DEVELOPING PATIENCE IS THE KEY

By recognizing the seasons of change in your life, you can learn to "forecast the weather," that is, you can monitor your feelings and understand that they are a natural result of your attempt to better your life. This should help you handle the process of change in a productive manner.

As you have learned by now, mastering change is a vital part of the Success Process. A primary virtue needed in this mastery is that of patience. You cannot rush the process of change; you have to allow it to unfold in the manner that is best suited to your nature. Patience is a very difficult virtue to acquire for many people, particularly men. In general, men want to take action. They don't want to wait for the action to unfold; they want to control it. A friend of mine once told me that he didn't have any concept of patience until his first child was born. "Then, I learned patience," he said.

It's true, you cannot rush the development of a child. After all the excitement and joy of the birth of a healthy child, there is a period of time, about six months, when the baby is totally helpless and dependent and, at the same time, does not have the ability to communicate or exhibit a great deal of response or reaction to the parents. It can be a difficult time for first-time parents because the wife is often still recovering from pregnancy and birth and the husband is often, to be kind, clueless as to what to do with himself.

My friend recalls a point when his newborn son was crying and would not stop. The sound of your helpless child crying and crying is heart-wrenching, and impossible to ignore. In a desperate effort to get his wailing son to sleep, my friend put him in the baby buggy, stuffed cotton in his own ears, and wheeled the infant around his apartment for several hours, trying to lull him to sleep. That was one way of enforcing patience.

You cannot rush the development of a child and you cannot

shortcut your way through the change process. Yet, many people have great difficulty dealing with changes. Even minor changes such as a different work schedule can throw them off. Larger changes can evoke even stronger feelings. Adults learn to expect changes such as death, illness, or disaster. These are part of life, and so we accept them even as we feel sadness, anger, or confusion. But sometimes negative feelings accompany even those changes that we willingly undertake in order to grow.

Changing jobs, changes in a relationship, moving to a new home, all such experiences can bring a wide range of conflicting feelings. Giving up the familiar for the unfamiliar can be difficult even when it means a better lifestyle overall. When you move to a new home, it may be a nicer place to live, but it means packing, unpacking, and reorienting yourself to the new environment. For children it can mean new schools and new classmates and new neighbors.

## MANAGING THE STRESS OF CHANGE

It is important to realize that when you make a change in your life, you will experience conflicting feelings. It is only natural, just as change itself is a natural part of life. The process of change can bring a great deal of stress into your life, even when the changes you are making will eventually have a positive impact on your life.

### FIVE TIPS FOR DEALING WITH THE STRESS OF CHANGE

*1. Stay focused on your dream for a better life.*

Sure, you may hit hard times when you make a change. People close to you may criticize you. You may doubt yourself. It may be exhausting to do all that is required to get to the next level of achievement or preparation. I never said it would be easy. But you can ease some of the stress by not focusing on *how hard it is*. Instead, keep in mind *how much better it will be* when you have completed this change.

## 2. Stay true to your principles and beliefs.

A great deal of stress can be triggered by actions that are not true to the beliefs and values and principles that have always guided your life. The process of change can test those basic beliefs, and occasionally, you may find that you have stepped outside the normal parameters within which you have generally lived your life. You may find yourself being untruthful or in other situations that you would not normally have to contend with. This can be highly stressful because you find yourself violating your own rules. Do your best to stay within your normal guidelines for behavior and you can avoid this stress, and be aware that stepping outside those guidelines will have serious and stressful repercussions.

## 3. Give yourself a break.

Understand that stress is going to accompany periods of change in your life, and compensate for that by giving yourself a break. Take time out from the usual routine to reduce stress and mental fatigue. Take walks in pleasant parks or in the countryside. Visit a small town, an island, the beach, a park, or anyplace where the pace of life is more relaxed. Do some sort of undemanding but useful volunteer work like picking up trash along a favorite river, or helping with a charity event to take your mind off your own problems and balance your view of the situation.

## 4. Unload your calendar.

This is not a time to be taking on more work or additional challenges that will add to your stress load. Back off a bit at work. Let someone else take on new projects until you have gotten a bit further along in the change process. Put off nonessential changes and other work for a while and focus on strengthening your resolve to better your life.

## 5. Put out your dis-stress signals.

Far too many people are unwilling to ask for help when they need to unload stress. Why invest in friendships and family relationships if you can't lean on them in hard times? I take it as a compliment when friends come to me when they need support. It makes me feel needed and valuable in their lives. You don't want to overdo it, but in critical times put out the signal that you need some support.

*Chapter 8*
# Build Your Dream Team

》》》》》》》》》》》

*Self-realization would not be achieved one by one, but all together or not at all.*

W. E. B. DuBois

THERE WAS A newspaper story recently about a farmer, Dan Foulk from central Illinois, whose spirit embodies the theme of this chapter. In the spring of 1996, Dan saw another man drowning in the swift current of the Spoon River, which goes through his land. The man had fallen out of a boat. His friends had made it to shore, but they had not been able to pull him out of the water. The drowning man was lucky, however, because Dan Foulk heard his cries.

Foulk knew the river, and he knew where he could safely walk through it even when it was swollen by flooding. While the drowning man's friends stood helplessly on the banks of the river, Foulk calmly took action to rescue him. "I just walked out to where he was—where the water was about up to my armpits—and told him to give me his hand and not to fight me," said the farmer. "I was just a little taller and a little bigger than him, I guess."

Sometimes, all it takes to save a life or change a life is someone just a little bigger, a little taller, a little more experienced and knowledgeable about the terrain; or simply someone who cares and is willing to listen or offer advice, or to give a pat on the back. We all need to be rescued from time to time, whether it is from real danger, or from those that we create in our minds.

We all need help in dealing with troubles and problems that we encounter as we try to better our lives. Building and maintaining mutually supportive relationships is essential if you are to successfully pursue a better life.

There are few things more valuable and more helpful in your journey along the Success Process than having a support team of trusted friends and family members. I believe that nobody makes it alone, and so your journey along the Success Process should not and really *cannot* be a solitary one.

## IT TAKES A TEAM TO PRODUCE A WINNER

Looking back, we have worked to:

- Increase your self-awareness so that you are in control of emotions and feelings that may have held you back in the past.
- Create a vision of your dreams and goals.
- Develop a plan to pursue those goals.
- Come up with your own Rules of the Road to stay focused on your plan without losing sight of the people and principles that are important to you.
- Take the risks necessary to move forward.
- Manage your responses to changes brought on by taking risks.

I do not expect you to do any of this without help. I believe that everything around us is designed as part of a universal mutual-support system. Scientists call this the *ecosystem*, in which every living thing, as well as the air, rock, dirt, and water around it, serves every other thing in some way. Philosophers express the same theory when they say that everything in the universe relates to everything else. The planets have a gravitational effect on one another, we have an impact on the lives of those around us. It is up to you to ensure that this impact is a positive and supportive one.

A key element of the Success Process is building relationships with people who care about you and believe in your goals as you grow and expand the possibilities for your life. Having relationships that strengthen you is vital. How many people do you know who have been urged on to succeed and to develop their talents by those people around them? I know many, many people like that. I also know people who have had difficulty building better lives for themselves because they didn't have anyone in their corner cheering them on, advising them, and helping them get through the hard times.

In my senior year at Middle Township High School, our basketball team went all the way to the state finals, even though we were a very small school. We did so well not because we had a lot of great individual players, but because we had a great *team*. There were other teams with more talented players; in fact, some of them had too much talent. On the teams loaded with good players, everybody wanted to be a star, rather than trying to fit in with their teammates.

We had a group of guys who were willing to do what was good for the team and our shared goals, rather than worrying about their individual statistics and achievements. Each of us trusted the other to do what was good for the team as a whole. Each of us worked to earn that trust in order to prove that we deserved to be part of the team. As a result, we achieved more *together* than we ever would have achieved if we each had played merely for personal glory or his own selfish purposes. We were bound together by mutual trust and respect and common goals, and so we were not only a basketball team; each of us was part of the *support team* for the other players.

There have been times in my own life when I didn't have that sort of support, and it is no surprise that I had difficulty achieving my goals during those periods. That is one reason I have been active in organizations that offer support to young people. Part of your responsibility as you pursue a better life is to help others learn the Success Process. While building your support team, I urge you to also become part of the support team for someone who may be a few steps back, or just starting out behind you. Do not become so focused on your own journey that you cannot stop occasionally and help others along the way. Each of us can make a great difference in the lives of other people, particularly as we move along the Success Process ourselves, growing in strength, gaining experience and knowledge.

## BEING A PART OF A TEAM

I am on the national board of Junior Achievement, which helps young people in kindergarten through grade school understand that there is a process for success in this country. Its focus is on nurturing partnerships between businesses and schools and the young people in them. It stresses the benefits and opportunities that exist in the business world. It offers hope for a better life, no matter what your circumstances are in the day-to-day world. This is a gang I wish every young person in America would join.

I love Junior Achievement because it frees people who otherwise may feel pinned down. My one great regret concerning JA, as it is known, is that it wasn't available to me as a boy growing up in Whitesboro. It would have opened my eyes and taught me about the Success Process so much earlier in my life. As it was, I was well into adulthood before I understood the value of developing a product or service, then marketing and selling it. I never understood management, or the real value of community service—lessons taught by Junior Achievement.

Founded seventy-five years ago, this global organization teaches young people how to be successful by teaching them how the world works. They learn economic principles and the American system of business. I'll never forget a young boy named Joseph whom I met through Junior Achievement. He came from a sadly typical inner-city background, where there are far more drive-by shootings than drive-in banks. Fortunately for Joseph, he had a one-woman support team: his grandmother. When Joseph was only eight or nine years old, his grandmother enrolled him in a much bigger team, Junior Achievement. Joseph still has a long fight ahead of him, but his grandmother and Junior Achievement have shown him a way to a better life. He knows that there is a better way. He knows there are opportunities out there, and they are accessible to him.

When I look back at those various times when I seemed to be stuck and going nowhere with my life, the one common denominator in every one of them was isolation. For one reason or another during these periods, I was separated from people I trusted, people I could lean on, people who understood me even when I did not understand myself. I've been reminded of those times in my life recently as I've tried to reach out to a family member who was struggling.

One of my goals is to help other members of my family and my extended family free themselves from the same burdens that hindered my development and growth for a time. My sister's daughter has had problems in school stemming from low self-esteem, and I've been working with her. She wanted to quit school so I tried to show her what a dead end that would lead her to. She is now back in the classroom and doing very well again. To a degree, she feels pressure from other kids because she is related to me, so I feel particularly responsible for supporting her through her difficult times as she tries to develop her own identity.

Forming and maintaining supportive, positive relationships not only is essential to your success, but it is also one of the most enjoyable and rewarding parts of life. We all need a team behind us to share in our victories and to help us overcome our defeats. In every aspect of life, whether it is in the home, at work, or in the community, we need people who share our vision for a better life.

## TEAMWORK IS A PART OF OUR HERITAGE

While some cynics might have you believe that human beings are a naturally suspicious and warring breed, many social scientists and historians can point to the golden eras of certain civilizations, in which cooperation and shared goals were the focal point. Recently, I visited Egypt and Turkey and I was profoundly affected by what I saw: the incredible achievements of the early civilizations in this part of the world. There are many striking examples of the power of human cooperation throughout the world, from the Roman aqueducts to the Great Wall of China.

It is true of the human race even today that in times of crisis, we come together regardless of our differences. Earthquakes, fires, mudslides, hurricanes and tornados, plane crashes, and other disasters create chaos that very often inspires heroic cooperative efforts of people from greatly different backgrounds. It has been noted before that when the terrible nuclear accident in Chernobyl occurred, in 1986, scientists and medical personnel from around the world rushed to help, and many continue to help today with the treatment of the widespread aftereffects on the people of that region of the world.

In recent years, prison inmates, who are generally regarded as the most antisocial of people, have volunteered to help fight flooding in the Midwest. The townspeople who have benefited from their labors, and often worked alongside them, have marveled at the transformations that occur in these outcasts when they are thrown into a cooperative effort for the good of others. I believe that in general, many people are seeking trusting relationships and mutually supportive relationships but they are fearful and cautious about being vulnerable to predators. The individualism and self-centeredness that pervade our society can make it difficult and sometimes dangerous to nurture personal relationships. I think this is one reason the chat rooms on the Internet are so popular. They allow people to reach out to others, while minimalizing the risk of rejection or the potential of abuse.

## BUILDING TRUST

How do you build and attract members to your support team as you work to create a better life for yourself? You start by proving your *trustworthiness* to others. Trust is not easily earned. Even a parent must prove his or her reliability to the child in order to earn trust. Real trust is established over time, through shared experiences and a pattern of reliability. Learning to trust others is a process that begins in childhood, within the confines of the family. Although a child may be blindly dependent at the start, even toddlers become wary of family members who prove to be unreliable or hurtful. If a child learns early on that his own parents and siblings cannot be trusted, odds are he will have difficulty establishing trusting relationships or being trustworthy himself, for the rest of his life.

Please note that I wrote of the importance of *being* trustworthy. Not *acting* trustworthy or *appearing* trustworthy, but *being* trustworthy. I can't tell you how many business, marketing, and sales books I have seen that have sections on *How to Win the Trust of* (name one here: customers, clients, co-workers, and so on). A few years ago, there was even some noise made about an effort to develop a cologne or perfume that would inspire trust. Guess who was behind the project? A Detroit car company.

Socrates must have seen the same sort of nonsense and insincerity in his time because he once offered this advice: *The way to gain a good reputation is to endeavor to be what you desire to appear.* In other words, you can't fake trustworthiness. Oh, you may fool a few people for a short period of time, but not for long. Appearances will get you only so far. There is a saying in golf about players who have all the right clothes and all the best equipment but can't play very well. It's said of such individuals, "He dresses par but plays like a hacker." You may fool some people at first, but once you step up to the tee, the truth is obvious.

There are all sorts of books that coach salesmen and others on how to appear trustworthy and sympathetic and honest, but in reality, having good character is the only way to earn the lasting trust and support of others. You don't just go out and buy good character. Nor do you develop it overnight. Again, it comes with a pattern of behavior, a way of living your life by certain rules based on age-old principles as basic but as enduring as the Golden Rule. Here are a few guidelines for building the sort of character that will deservedly earn you the trust and respect of others.

## Eleven Character Traits That Inspire Trust

### 1. *Do what you say you will do.*

It is amazing how many people and even big businesses fail to live up to their promises, but still expect people to trust them. Again, you may fool some people for a while, but eventually the crowds will thin, and you'll be left making false promises to thin air. On the other hand, if you consistently live up to the expectations that you create, you may have to build an arena to accommodate the crowds that want to line up on your side. When your actions follow your words, you don't have to work to impress people or to win them over. In time, they will see the strength of your character and line up to be on your support team. If you consistently do not make good on your word, however, you will be one of those people who specializes in short-term friendships, skipping from person to person, crowd to crowd, as people grow weary of your deceptions and unreliability.

## 2. Listen without judgment.

There is no greater favor you can do for someone than to be a devoted and trusted listener. Not an adviser or counselor, simply a listener. Give the speaker your full attention and allow him or her to state the situation or express the emotions based on his or her perceptions. Don't interrupt, don't be distracted, don't try to formulate your answers and thoughts while the speaker is talking. Listen without judgment and let the speaker find the way.

## 3. Be there.

A friend told me that he recently filled in for a neighbor couple who had to leave town on the night of their son's school recital. He knew this boy, a second-grader, fairly well, but had not spent a great deal of time alone with him. He did know, however, that it was important for the boy to have a familiar face in the crowd since his own parents were out of town. The boy didn't say much on the way to the recital, nor did he acknowledge that it mattered that this fellow was going to stay and watch him perform with his class. But when he took the stage with all of his classmates, the first thing that boy did was scan the crowd for his neighbor's face. When he saw it, he lit up. The neighbor was where he said he would be. Trust was established, and it was visible in that boy's eyes. The significant thing here is that, although the neighbor did not have to step in for the parents, he had the insight and instincts to see how important it would be to the boy. That says more about the character of this neighbor than any claims he might make.

### 4. *Pay what you owe when it is due.*

This sounds almost revolutionary in a time of credit cards and delayed-payment plans, but in personal transactions there is nothing that builds trust faster than paying debts promptly and paying for services when they are rendered.

### 5. *Act honorably even in the face of temptation or criticism.*

It is easy to be an honorable person if there is no temptation, or if your honor is never challenged. But how honorable are you in doing your expense reports or in reporting your income at tax time? I know people who cheat and lie in these situations, and brag openly about it. I also know that I would never trust these people in a critical situation because their *honor* runs no deeper than a scratch. The most important thing is to be honest with yourself first. Ask yourself if you are comfortable with your own level of integrity. It is vital to demonstrate integrity, to stand up for your beliefs, and to resist pressure to do what you know to be wrong.

### 6. *Tell the truth about yourself and others.*

I read a report the other day that said lying on résumés is so widespread today that many employers take it for granted. I don't understand this at all. How can an employer trust someone who has lied about something so important as his or her education and previous experience? Would you want to work for someone who would hire a liar?

To attract the trust of others, it is also vital to always be truthful in regard to other people. If you are known to tell lies about other people, why should anyone want to associate with you? They know they will be setting themselves up for your untruthful portrayals.

## 7. *Guard what is entrusted to you.*

In trusting relationships, people share their greatest fears or most embarrassing moments because they trust each other. To do this with someone you do not know well is to expose yourself to the risk of being criticized or rejected. I read recently of a high school boy who told his most trusted friend a secret. It was an extremely private matter, but this friend did not guard it as he should have. He told someone else, and within a few days the boy's secret was out not only in the high school, but throughout the community. As a result, he was taunted and even threatened, and eventually, he had to leave the high school one year before graduation, all because his friend had betrayed his trust.

## 8. *Be a source of strength.*

It may sound contradictory, but if you want to have people to lean on in your troubled times, you have to provide a source of strength to them when they are in need. No one is strong all the time, and even the weakest of us has the power to provide support to those who trust and rely on us to be there for them.

## 9. *Acknowledge your mistakes.*

This too sounds strange, but the person who is willing to admit mistakes and imperfections is more likely to inspire confidence than one who never acknowledges being wrong or having weaknesses. The three most difficult words for some people to say are

*I don't know.* Who do you trust more, the person who always has an answer, or the one who acknowledges the limits of his or her experience and training?

## 10.  *Share your blessings without looking for praise or payment.*

I am active in many charitable organizations, and at their functions and fund-raisers I can always tell within a short time who is there to do good as opposed to who is there to look good. Now, it is true, working with charities can be a great way to meet energetic and powerful people, but if you go into it for that reason you will quickly be spotted as an opportunist, and someone whose motives will always be mistrusted. Do good deeds without looking for rewards, and the rewards will probably find you anyway.

## 11.  *Put the welfare of others before your own.*

How many people do you know who are genuinely more interested in seeing others succeed than in promoting themselves for success? How about equally interested in the successes of others as well as their own success? If you can come up with more than a handful of names, you have a remarkable circle of acquaintances. And you undoubtedly have a lot of people whom you have trusting relationships with. To engender trust, show that you are at least as concerned about other people as you are about yourself.

## WALKING THE WALK

A good appearance and outward charms may attract people, but they stick around only if they come to believe that what lies within you is worthy of their trust. Teammates practice and play together to build trust. Soldiers are trained together as combat units in order to build trust. Romantic relationships begin with dating and getting to know each other. Friendships begin with conversations and the sharing of mutual interests. Trust is one of the most essential ingredients to relationships of any kind, but it is also generally the aspect of a relationship that takes the longest time to establish. Trust is what holds a relationship together over the long term. But it can be a fragile entity, one that must be carefully maintained and never taken for granted.

Trust is established only if your actions are consistent with your words. You have to live it to earn it, you can't just say it. That is why the slow building of trust is so important to relationships. When you are building a support team, you have to be patient in choosing your partners. You should only place as much trust in them as they have proven worthy of. I know that can be difficult, but as that teenage boy discovered, some people simply cannot bear the burden of trust.

Successful relationships and successful business partnerships are based upon trust and a shared sense that you can depend on each other even in hard times. Trust is knowing that your teammate, whether in business, personal, or community matters, has the required strength of character, a sense of honor and truthfulness, and abilities to support you.

When you trust those around you, you feel more confident and able to manage the Success Process. It is like having a safety net. You know that if you stumble, there will be someone there that you trust to at least cushion your fall and get you back up and on track again. These people also serve as your reality check. They let you know when you don't know what you don't know.

Having trust in your support teammates means that you know they will not put their self-interest above your best interest. Make a list of the people on your team, those whom you trust to guard prized possessions, to protect your privacy, to keep a secret, and to tell the truth no matter what. Next to each name, write down what makes each of them trustworthy.

_____          _____

_____          _____

_____          _____

_____          _____

Now, write down the names of people who might trust *you* in similar situations and what characteristics *you* have that make you trustworthy to each of them.

_____          _____

_____          _____

_____          _____

_____          _____

Are the same names on both lists? How did it feel to consider whom you trust and who trusts you? Was it difficult or easy to identify what it is about another person that results in your trusting him or her? What about identifying your own characteristics that result in others trusting you—was that easy or difficult to do, and how did it make you feel?

There is a certain amount of risk involved in trusting others. The decision to trust has the potential for both positive and negative consequences, and those consequences depend on how your team members respond to situations as you progress along the Success Process. Not all relationships involve the same degree of trust, but trust is the key to building relationships and support teams.

Before I started my new business, I spent months and months first building a team. I have allied myself with some of the best marketing, advertising, writing, and sales people because I know that with a great team behind me, I can do more than I ever might do on my own. When I began building my business team, I looked for people who were *hungry* and not afraid to work. Mostly, though, I was looking for people of character whom I could trust.

One of the biggest problems I face on a day-to-day basis is trusting people to be honest with me. People often come to me with hidden agendas, though often they are not hidden very well. It happens every day, often several times a day. Mere acquaintances or perfect strangers contact my office in hopes of making the connection. Sometimes they mask it well, pretending that they are interested in doing business with me and my associates, or with one of the charities I am involved with.

I think I have developed a pretty keen eye for the sneaky opportunists out there. I'm sure it is the same with most celebrities or influential people, whether the person is a CEO or a supervisor, a U.S. senator or a precinct committeeman. In truth, everyone has to develop the ability to read others and to read their motives. Naturally, each individual has an agenda, a personal goal that may or may not be compatible with yours. You can't expect every person out there to give your concerns and goals priority over his or hers. They key is to find people whose goals are *compatible* with yours.

It is simply a matter of being able to determine the proper level of trust to place in someone, and to come to a quick assessment of whether their motives are compatible with your own goals.

## FORGING POSITIVE PARTNERSHIPS

Relationships are critical to your ability to achieve your goals, but only those that are positive and make you stronger. Some partnerships are more successful than others. Identify a positive relationship you have had that has helped you pursue past goals.

Your positive teammate was:

_____

Identify one thing that worked well in this relationship. Possible responses might include:

- We got along well.
- My teammate was very supportive.
- We communicated well.
- We were always able to solve problems.
- We agreed on what we should do and how we were going to do it.
- We trusted each other completely.
- We agreed on what was most important.

_____

_____

Identify one thing that did not work well in the relationship. Possible responses might be:

- We couldn't agree on what to do.
- We had very different methods.
- I didn't feel trustful of this teammate.
- I had to do all the work.
- We didn't communicate very well.

_____

_____

Looking at past experiences with partnerships can help you learn how to build successful relationships in the future. Successful alliances between individuals often have common characteristics. These characteristics can be found in cooperative efforts that work well regardless of the context of the relationship, whether a family, friends, a sports team, a surgical team, an automobile factory, or a musical group. In fact, musical groups serve as outstanding examples of teams in which mutual support is essential to overall success. Whether you are listening to the Chicago Symphony, a local garage band, or a street-corner quartet, when a musical group is working in perfect harmony the result is, well, perfect harmony.

## Five Key Characteristics for Successful Teamwork

### 1. Commitment to a common goal.

The first key is agreement on goals between those involved. If you don't share the same goals, it would be impossible to decide how to work together to achieve them. I wouldn't bring someone onto my team in my business if their goal for the business was different from mine, just as the Chicago Symphony Orchestra wouldn't hire the rock drummer from Def Leppard to lead its percussion section. Different goals, bad harmony.

It is important to make sure that all members of your support team understand your goals. Confusion over goals is often a major source of conflict and misunderstanding between individuals on a team or in partnerships. In your journey along the Success Process, you don't want to team up with someone whose vision for your life is vastly different from yours. In your relationships, if you see that pursuing your goals is going to require a great deal of travel, you don't want to get involved with someone who will resent that. In your business, if your goal is to have a broad-based sports and event marketing business, you don't bring in a consultant whose expertise is in agriculture. Of course, the differences can be more subtle. Often in business, partnerships fail when those involved come to a crossroads in the development of their business and then can't agree on which path to take. That is why it is important at the very outset of a relationship to develop mutual understanding and shared commitments to the final goals.

## 2. *Common values and expectations.*

People on winning teams share common expectations about appropriate behavior by all of those involved. This includes agreement about such things as what each of the parties can depend on the others for, how personal their conversations will be, what role each member of the team is expected to play, and so on. When you put together your team, whether it is comprised of family members and friends helping you reach personal goals or business associates working with you toward career and professional goals, you have to know exactly what each member will contribute, just as members of the Chicago Bulls or New York Knicks have to know and trust that each team member will fulfill his individual role as well as contributing toward the team effort.

In musical groups, the rules or direction for the team are provided by the notes or musical score. On your team and in your personal partnerships the rules and direction must be set by you and the other team members. Agreements about expected behavior in the relationship are based upon the values held by members of the group. Those who hold greatly differing values are likely to have very different ideas about appropriate behavior in the relationship. While no two individuals agree exactly on every issue, it is difficult to maintain a lasting relationship or a viable team when the individuals involved have substantially differing values regarding matters vital to the stated goals and objectives.

## 3. Complementary roles.

In the same way that musicians must decide which instrument each will play and which part each of the vocalists will sing, people involved in successful partnerships have a clear understanding of what part each will play in achieving their mutually agreed upon goals.

Clarity about roles is essential. It gives each of those involved on your team the information he or she needs about how each fits into the game plan, what they can expect from one another, and how their roles interact. If each participant's role is not clearly defined, conflict is inevitable.

## 4. A shared plan for confronting and solving problems.

Conflict is a part of life. Whenever two or more individuals are engaged in a relationship, disagreements are likely to occur. The challenge in building your team and the relationships within it is to find ways of resolving differences of opinion or other conflicts so that the relationships and the team always move forward, rather than getting hung up on internal problems. Can you imagine a musical performance in which members of the band stop playing because they can't get agreement on how to interpret a song? How about a basketball team so torn apart by jealousies and misunderstandings that they can't compete? Fortunately, there are steps that can be followed in working out conflict in team relationships.

### A. Define the problem.
The first step in resolving conflict is to decide together what exactly the problem is by identifying areas of both disagreement and agreement.

*B. Diagnose the causes.*
Next, it is important to understand what events and actions led to the conflict. Sometimes it helps to bring in a neutral third party to help the participants unravel and sort through conflicting information.

*C. Generate possible solutions.*
Identify possible mutually desired goals for resolution of the conflict and actions each person can take to achieve the resolution.

*D. Decide on a mutually acceptable solution.*
Evaluate the effects of implementing each of the possible solutions identified and what cooperative efforts and information would be required. Select the option most acceptable to the parties.

*E. Implement the solution.*
Once the parties involved have agreed on a solution, they should all be involved in implementing it.

*F. Evaluate the results.*
All parties involved should join in evaluating the effectiveness and efficiency of the solution to see if it resolved the problem; if not, another solution should be sought.

## 5. *A way to evaluate progress.*

It is one thing to know where you are going or to have a common goal, but successful partnerships require also that you have a way to evaluate whether progress is being made, and how much progress is being made. Successful teammates agree upon the goal itself so that advance toward it can be measured.

## COMMUNICATING WITH YOUR SUPPORT TEAM

All trusting relationships begin with good communication. If someone is difficult to talk with, if they don't appear to be listening to you or responding to you, there is a pretty good chance that the relationship is not going anywhere. But the relationship clicks when communication is there. When the first date ends with both of you talking late into the night, or the first business meeting extends well beyond the planned period of time, it is because lines of communication were clear and the comfort level high. Those experiences frequently end with one of the party saying something like this: I feel like we've known each other for years.

Communication, like trust and trustworthiness, is vital to developing relationships that will support you in your search for a better life. The quality of the relationship is affected by the quality of the communication between those involved. Relationships deepen or fall apart based upon the level of communication. Inevitably, there will be misunderstandings and miscommunications in almost any relationship, but there are ways to minimize those problems and to heighten your communications skills, which are sometimes referred to as interpersonal skills.

We all have had experiences in which we misunderstood someone, or someone misunderstood what we have said. The problem is that communication is a process that involves a common set of symbols, signs, or behavior, but these are interpreted and filtered through our own individual experiences and perceptions. Miscommunication can result also from the fact that messages may be sent verbally, or through expression and body language, or in the way we act. Nonverbal messages are most often misinterpreted. Ineffective communication is a great barrier to establishing productive partnerships and building your team because successful teams depend on common understandings of goals, roles, rules, and so on.

If members of a musical group do not communicate effectively, if they all play in different keys, discord results. To help you stay in the same key with members of your support team, you need to work at effective communication. Sports teams and musical groups practice, practice, practice to sharpen communication between members.

Social scientists say that 25 percent of us are poor at verbal communication and that 63 percent do not give verbal direction well. Their research has found that from 50 to 70 percent of people fear speaking in public. Poor writing skills plague not only modern businesses, but colleges and universities, where instructors can't decipher the work of their students. The truth is that even many people who think they are good communicators are not. Think about people whom you regard to be good leaders, whether a prominent national figure or someone within your own circle of friends and co-workers. I'll wager that among the things each of those leaders has in common is the ability to communicate well, whether in writing, in one-on-one conversation, or when speaking to a group.

Consider also the value of communication skills in the media. Even Michael Jordan would admit that a sizeable portion of his success off the basketball court as a spokesman for a wide range of commercial enterprises is due to his communication skills.

Communication is not just a way of getting along in life. It is at the heart of life. Look at its role in relation to your Success Circles. It is crucial to your ability to establish and maintain relationships. It is absolutely critical in your job and career. You can never expand your role in the community if you can't communicate with those around you. Using words well, as Oliver Wendell Holmes once said, is "like putting skin on a living thought." Yet, so many people today enter the job market without mastering the basics by learning to read well, to think well, to write well, and to speak well. If you haven't achieved at least a reasonable level of skill in those four areas, I suggest you seek ways to polish them up. The world is not waiting for you or for anyone. The fax line is ringing, the cellular phones are lit up. Something has just come over the modem. CNN has the latest.

Today, communication shapes our lives. It influences our actions and those of people around us. If you want to change your life, if you want to pursue a better life, effective communication is critical.

It may seem ironic, but even as the world moves more and more to technology and electronic communication, the power to communicate well is increasingly valued. If you can't state your ideas in a coherent and concise manner, it does you no good to have e-mail at your fingertips. No amount of high-tech equipment can mask poor communication skills. Technology has given us the ability to communicate instantaneously with people throughout the world. It is breaking down the boundaries that have historically separated us. It is hastening the development of a global village, in which we are in constant and immediate reach of almost anyone anyplace in the world.

We are constantly being told that we have entered the dawn of the information age, in which the greatest rewards will go to those who have the most information most swiftly at their command. Your support team will grow in this environment to include hundreds, thousands, even millions of people and resources, if you develop the vital communication skills. This means being able to communicate not only verbally and in writing, but also on the Internet. This too is part of the Success Process. Banks, libraries, universities, all of these sources of knowledge are increasingly calling upon those who use them to have advanced technological communications skills. When the eighth-century monks devised the first clock as a way to know when to pray, they did not comprehend that this invention would one day play such a major role in the lives of most of the human race. High-tech, high-speed communication skills are essential if you are to pursue a better life.

## GROWING YOUR SUPPORT TEAM

Relationships require good communication and they also require maintenance. If you take them for granted, they will wither and die. If you abuse them, they will disintegrate. To build a trusting relationship, you need to be mindful of these maintenance tips.

### 1. *Be the host, not the guest, in the relationship.*

When you invite someone into your home, you practice good manners and social grace by attending to their needs and being mindful of their comfort. The same should hold true when you invite someone into your life in a relationship, whether it is a business relationship or a personal one. Understand the other person's interests, needs, and point of view. Inquire into developments in his or her life rather than opening every conversation with what has occurred in yours. Be alert to significant events and changes in the other person's life. Build trust by showing that you want to be an active force in that person's life.

### 2. *Pay attention to the details.*

A couple I know visited the home of a famous person a few months ago. The host wined and dined my friends graciously, but what impressed my friends the most was the little things that this host did. "She personally put together a tray of goodies for our nightstand, and saw to it that we had comfortable pillows," my friends reported. "She seemed to take a great deal of pride and interest in being a good host." It is the little things that often make the greatest impression, and when you are building a trusting relationship, attention to the details can mean a lot. Remember special occasions, birthdays and anniversaries, the names of children and pets. Do it because you are truly involved and interested, because that is the only way to build trust.

### 3. *Honor all commitments, big and small, spoken and unspoken.*

Few things can build trust, or tear it down, as quickly as the keeping, or failing to keep, commitments. If you intend to build a trusting relationship with someone, you had better be prepared to be there when you say you will be there, when you said you would be there. You had better be prepared also to honor the unspoken commitments. When my father died recently, the people I trust and depend on the most stepped forward. I did not have to ask for their support. There was no spoken commitment that they would be there for me in times of sadness in my life, but I knew they would be there and they were. Those people have made a commitment to our relationship that is based on far more than their own self-interest.

### 4. *Live up to your own expectations.*

You cannot expect people to invest more in their relationship with you than you are willing to invest in your relationship with them. If you don't remember their birthdays, don't expect them to send a cake for yours. If you don't show up to celebrate their victories and successes or to console them in their setbacks, don't expect them to rush to your side on your own occasions. Have you ever known someone who expected others to live by rules and principles that he or she openly ignored? That is what I am referring to when I say that you should live up to your own expectations. If you expect members of your team to live with integrity, you had better be a model of it yourself. No one wears away trust as quickly as someone who does not practice what he preaches.

### 5. *Admit your mistakes.*

It is going to happen. You will do something thoughtless or reckless that hurts your relationship with someone who has trusted you and been there for you. The worst thing you can do is to take someone on your support team for granted and simply assume that they will give you the benefit of the doubt. No. As I noted earlier, trust is earned with trustworthy action. If you screw up, if you hurt someone or your relationship with someone through thoughtless action, go to that person you have wronged and make it right. Otherwise, don't expect the relationship to continue.

## Chapter 9

# Win by a Decision

>>>>>>>>>>

ROBERT EARL LOVE was a tall and skinny child, and always so *hungry* that his friends called him "Butterbean." He grew up with thirteen other family members in a two-bedroom house in Bastrop, Louisiana. In order to keep from getting lost in that crowd, Butterbean attached himself to a favorite uncle, who took him everywhere. That uncle loved Butterbean and the child loved him. The boy loved him so much that he mimicked his uncle's speech impediment, a very bad stutter. People thought it was cute at first, and most figured Butterbean would grow out of it. He surely did grow—to a height of six feet, eight inches—but his uncle's stutter stayed with him.

The speech impediment frustrated him, but Butterbean was able to release his frustrations on the basketball court. Butterbean spoke with great difficulty, but he was a graceful athlete. His basketball skills earned him a scholarship at tiny Southern University, where he was said to be among the best small-college players in the nation. His stuttering kept him from selling himself as a commanding presence to NBA scouts, despite his 30 points a game average in college. He was drafted late for a player of his skills, in the fourth round by the Cincinnati Royals. He played just two seasons for them, and then was cut. Butterbean ended up taking a part-time job in a hospital and playing in basketball's backwater of that era, the old Eastern League, for $50 a game.

In the long run, Butterbean's athletic ability could not be denied, however, and he eventually made it into the NBA, where he bounced around for several years as a backup player until the Chicago Bulls got him in 1968 as part of a trade for a player thought to be much better. Butterbean, who was then twenty-six, was considered more or less just a throw-in on the deal, and the Bulls tried to trade him away even before he'd moved to town. But Butterbean stayed, and he became one of the greatest players in the team's history.

For seven straight seasons, Bob "Butterbean" Love led the Bulls in scoring while also earning a reputation as one of the toughest defensive players in the league. While he had long dreamed of proving himself through his basketball, Love later said that his real dream all those years was that he would start to speak "and the words would just flow out of my mouth."

Even as a star player for the Chicago Bulls, Bob Love was rarely asked to make public appearances or to give interviews because of his tortured speech. It would often take him minutes to get one word out. When his athletic career ended, Butterbean could not find meaningful work because of his speech impediment.

A proud man, he was forced eventually to take work as a busboy and dishwasher, where, instead of feeling demeaned, he endeavored to be "the best dishwasher and busboy" he could be. His hard work won him praise, but his bosses told him that he would never be promoted because of his inability to speak. No longer able to rely on his athletic skills, Butterbean might have spent the rest of his life in that lowly work, but at the age of forty-five, at the urging of people who cared about him, he made a decision to pursue a better life.

Butterbean went to a speech therapist and applied hard work and dedication to pursuing a vision for himself. He had one more dream to fulfill. Many people who knew him doubted that Bob Love could ever overcome his speech impediment, particularly when he had gotten such a late start at speech therapy. But he did it.

Bob Love's uniform jersey with number 10 hangs in the Chicago Bulls' United Center, and Butterbean is still hanging around too, now as a goodwill ambassador for the team. It is a job that demands that he travel around the city and the country speaking to adults and children in large groups. He does it joyfully, and although he says he still has to work to overcome his speech impediment, most of the time the words really do flow out of his mouth.

Bob Love is an example of what you can do when you make a decision to pursue a better life even when it would appear that there is nothing you can do, even when you have had failures in the past, even when your life appears to be at a dead end. The ability to make the decision to change your life for the better is crucial to the Success Process. If you can't bring yourself to make decisions and to take action, you will never be able to break free and create opportunities where none appeared to exist.

## DECISIONS, DECISIONS, DECISIONS

Up to this point, I have offered steps to help you:

- Increase your self-awareness so that you are in control of emotions and feelings that may have held you back in the past.
- Create a vision of your dreams and goals.
- Develop a plan to pursue those goals.
- Come up with your own Rules of the Road to stay focused on your plan without losing sight of the people and principles that are important to you.
- Take the risks necessary to move forward.

- Manage your responses to changes brought on by taking risks.
- Build a support team to assist you in dealing with changes in your life.

Even if they have mastered all of the steps listed above, many people falter in their efforts to seek a better life because they have difficulty making decisions. It's not that they don't have goals and a vision for where they want to go, or that they don't have a plan, or that they lack courage to take risks and make changes. It's simply that they don't have a method for making good decisions, and that can be a disastrous shortcoming.

Some people are afraid to make decisions because they are afraid to move from what is known into the unknown. Some fear the decision-making process because it exposes them to criticism and evaluation. They don't want to be wrong, ever. Decision-making is such an important skill, yet we receive little training in how to go about it thoughtfully.

What you are in this world is largely the result of the decisions you have made so far in life. That's right, *your* decisions. No one else can make the important decisions for you, and no one else *should* make them for you. You are not the victim of circumstances that happen *to* you, you are the maker of decisions that can work *for* you. You are free to make your decisions. You have that right. You have the power to choose by making decisions. If you are not happy with where you are in life, or if you think you can do better, then you can choose to make a decision.

One of the best decisions I ever made was to leave one of the best jobs I've ever had. Life is about making choices, choosing paths, and all of our life we struggle with making the right decisions. I see life as a series of paths taken and paths not taken, and if you don't develop a consistent method for choosing yours, you will surely waste precious time and effort. As director of education at the federal prison in Chicago, I was in a position to make a tremendous impact on the lives of men who had made many poor choices in the past. It was a challenging, tough, and constantly stimulating job. Believe me, federal prison inmates do not give you any opportunity to coast. They are always challenging you, prodding around your mind for signs of weakness or for an opening to somehow get one up on you.

It was a game, but not one that you could afford to take lightly. It was like a chess game, with far more serious consequences. There were many aspects of that job that I enjoyed, and the opportunity for advancement was good, but other opportunities were opening up for me too. I had met Bob Brown through mutual friends, and he introduced me to his incredible network in public relations and marketing. As a former assistant to the President of the United States, Bob was wired into the highest levels of business and politics. I knew that working with him would expand my horizons, and even though I was giving up a great deal of job security, I made the decision to make a career switch. It opened up an entire new world of opportunity to me. It put me in a position to pair my lifelong interest in sports with my growing interest in business. At the time, though, it was an extremely difficult decision to make. I had not learned at the time to master the *Five Steps to Winning by Decision* that I am going to teach you in this chapter.

How do you know if you are making good decisions in your life? Here are some characteristics of good decisions:

- Good decisions open opportunities.
- Good decisions make you feel good about yourself.
- Good decisions allow you to express your talents, skills, and knowledge.
- Good decisions silence your critics.
- Good decisions move you closer to your goals.
- Good decisions cause you to always look to the future.
- Good decisions reduce your frustrations and anger.

- Good decisions increase your potential.
- Good decisions attract dynamic people to your cause.
- Good decisions are a magnet for wealth.

How do you know you are making bad decisions? Here are some characteristics of bad decisions:

- Bad decisions put you on a dead-end street.
- Bad decisions result in second thoughts.
- Bad decisions cause you to look over your shoulder.
- Bad decisions inspire feelings of regret.
- Bad decisions are a lure for critics.
- Bad decisions bring cynicism.
- Bad decisions attract predators who hope to capitalize on more bad decisions.
- Bad decisions are a lure for misfortune.

Obviously, if you want to pursue a better life, you need a process and a method for making better decisions, a process that uses all of your creative and analytical powers, all the resources at your command. Big decisions require big thinking. Often, the only difference between you and someone you admire is that they have made the decision to make their lives better. There is a traditional African proverb that says, "If it is to be, it's up to me." Judith Jamison was writing about taking responsibility for decisions when she wrote, *The stars are in the sky. And I'm a person. I have a God-given talent, but I'm still that person, just like you, with two arms and two legs, and I decided to take it someplace."*

Napoleon Hill, author of the classic *Think and Grow Rich*, has noted that successful people make decisions quickly and firmly once they have reviewed all the information available. Unsuccessful people, he said, make decisions slowly and change them often. He claimed also that ninety-eight out of a hundred people never make up their minds about their major purpose in life because *they simply can't make a decision and stick with it*. I hope to help you change that percentage by becoming one of those people who can make good life decisions.

One of the biggest obstacles to the decision-making process is something I am very familiar with: procrastination. I come from a long line of procrastinators. It might have been longer, but they kept putting off having more of us. Some say that not making a decision is a decision in itself, one with many implications. I've worked at overcoming my tendency to procrastinate, which is the tendency to put things off. One in five Americans is a chronic procrastinator, according to DePaul University professor Joseph R. Ferrari, co-author of *Procrastination and Task Avoidance: Theory, Research and Treatment.* Ferrari has identified two types of procrastinators: the *arousal* type and the *avoidance* type. The first kind of procrastinator puts things off because they get a thrill out of doing things at the buzzer and in a last-minute rush. The second type puts things off to avoid them for a wide number of reasons ranging from fear of failure to simply wanting to avoid doing something they consider to be unpleasant. Those who procrastinate because they have a fear of failure believe that they are better off not trying than trying and failing. Mark Twain was the literary hero of procrastinators. His motto was *"Never put off till tomorrow what you can do the day after tomorrow."*

Here are a few other common phrases you'll hear from serious procrastinators:

- This just isn't the right time to make that decision.
- I have a few other important matters to deal with first.
- My schedule just won't give me the time for that matter.
- I've been meaning to get to that.
- I'll tackle that when I've got more experience.
- You wouldn't believe all the stuff I have to clear off my desk before I can get to that.
- Tomorrow, I promise you.

- I just have to get away from all the distractions to focus on that.
- I'm waiting to make a bigger move.
- There is probably a safer way of doing this. I'll wait for it.

Do any of those sound familiar to you? Procrastinators are creative in making excuses, even if they can't do anything else. The question they always get from people around them is "What are you waiting for?" A friend of mine who has children is always mocking parental procrastinators, couples who say, *We're waiting for the right time to start our family.* Good luck. There is no *perfect time* to start a family. You will never feel you have enough in the bank or enough free time to start having children. But believe me, once you start having them, you will find the money and you will find the time.

Decision-making gridlock is a serious problem if you are interested in pursuing your vision for a better life. Often, it is based in fear, whether your particular brand is fear of success or fear of failure or just fear of pulling your head out of the ground (or from wherever you might have stuck it). Think about the successful people you know. Are any of them procrastinators? Do they spend days looking before they leap? Or do they go after what they want? I was going to come up with a list to help you overcome this problem but . . . just kidding.

The self-defeating habit of procrastination is a fairly common trait. There are three theories as to why you put things off that are vitally important:

1. You are just lazy.
2. You are self-destructive.
3. You like being stuck because it brings you sympathy.

As you can tell, these theories do not paint a pretty picture of the procrastinator's personality. None of them really explains the problem or deals with it in a very logical manner. No one is born lazy. Only truly demented people enjoy causing pain and mental torment to themselves. Sympathy may be one form of attention, but it is hardly uplifting or inspiring.

Recent studies of procrastination have found that people who put things off as a matter of habit are often troubled with feelings of hopelessness, low self-esteem, guilt, or fear. Procrastination is also the province of perfectionists, who put things off because they are waiting for the perfect time to produce the perfect results.

Here are a few tips to help my fellow procrastinators out there get beyond their "but's" and past their "one day I'm gonna's."

## EIGHT SMALL STEPS FOR GETTING PAST PROCRASTINATION

### 1. Take small bites.

Have you ever been to one of those Mexican restaurants that advertise *Burritos As Big As Your Head*? They aren't exaggerating, much. But you don't order one and then say, "I think I'll wait for a better time to eat this." No, you get to work on it. You don't try to do it in one huge bite, however; you eat that giant burrito one small bite at a time. This is not only good for digestion, it is good for decision-making.

### 2. Begin now!

Without even giving yourself time to think of excuses, sit down now and start the process and force yourself to keep at it for at least an hour. Set a time to pick up where you left off.

### 3. Slam the door on critics.

If you feel that you can't make a decision because someone is holding you back, break free of that sense of helplessness and victimization. Sometimes you have to go against the sentiments of those around you in order to make decisions that open opportunities for yourself. You can't expect others to always share your vision. Don't let anything or anyone stand between you and your freedom to make decisions that improve your life. It is simply impossible to always reach a consensus.

## 4. Lighten up.

Procrastinators tend to take themselves far too seriously. You are significant only within a very limited scope. The world is not focused on your every move. The sun will still come up tomorrow. The stars will still shine tonight. No matter what you do, the future of the galaxy is not resting on your shoulders. If the thought of making a decision is weighing so heavily that you can't make it, you need to step away and regain perspective so that you don't take yourself so seriously. Do something to take your mind off the decision and to lighten your mood. Take a walk, visit a friend who cheers you up, read a comic novel, or take in a comedy at the movie theater or on television. Get out of that dark mood.

## 5. Think of the carrot, not the stick.

Those who put things off sometimes do it because they focus on the difficulties and demands of taking an action rather than on the rewards that await them. Focus on the solution, not the problem. Keep your mind on the rewards and results of your decision rather than on the process itself. After all, how many times have you fretted and worried about doing something, only to discover that it was not nearly as painful as you had imagined? Don't dream of all the work involved; dream of the rewards you will reap when you have taken action and gone after what you want from life.

## 6. *Bring in a coach.*

These days people have personal fitness trainers, personal bankers, personal speech coaches, personal accountants, personal nutrition advisers. Why not bring in a friend or family member to be your anti-procrastination coach? Give them a list of the things you need to do and order them to dog you until you do them. Provide the whip if you feel it is necessary. Drastic procrastination calls for drastic action.

## 7. *Live in the moment.*

I knew of a fellow who came to the end of his life and realized that he had accomplished nothing that he had wanted to do. He lamented this fact to a friend of his, saying, *I don't know how I wasted my whole life.* The friend observed that he hadn't started out to waste his whole life. First, he had wasted a minute of it, then an hour, then a day, then a week, a month, a year, a decade, and *then* his whole life. Take a clue, and do the opposite. Use up every minute, every hour, every day, until you have made the most of your entire life.

## 8. *Don't demand perfection.*

Tell yourself there is not going to be a *perfect* time to get started, and that you don't have to be *perfect* in your performance. Compromise and start immediately and rough out the task, and then build upon it. No one is standing over your shoulder demanding that you make no mistakes. This is a problem I have. Because I spent so much of my life trying to prove my value and worth and to elevate my family's image, I became a perfectionist. It's funny, but trying to always be perfect often results in your not getting much of anything done. The pressure that perfectionists put on themselves is so intense that they can't possibly be perfect at all the things they set out to do; as a result, they get stuck. Believe me, I know. I am constantly telling myself to ease up, and to just take each task step by step, without fear that someone will criticize my work. This perfectionism was the main impediment to my own efforts to make good decisions to better my life. A lot of times we make things more difficult for ourselves by placing this sort of undue pressure on ourselves. You are far more likely to succeed if you work to please yourself, without feeling pressured to meet the standards of others.

## MAKING GOOD DECISIONS A HABIT

Before I introduce my decision-making process to you, I want to get you thinking about your own decision-making habits. You probably haven't given much thought to them because you make so many decisions in your life that the process becomes automatic, until you come up on a really difficult decision such as changing jobs, committing to a relationship, or taking on a position of leadership in your community. Think for a moment about all the decisions you have made in the last twenty-four hours.

I'll bet you have decided, consciously or unconsciously, things such as:

- When to get out of bed.
- What to wear.
- What to have for breakfast.
- The best route to work.
- What tasks to undertake at work.
- What to do after work.
- When to go to bed.

Along with those humdrum daily decisions, you undoubtedly made countless other small decisions—what color shoes or tie to choose—and, perhaps, even some much bigger, more important decisions such as whether to buy a new car this year, or to wait. When you begin to think about it, it is striking how many decisions we make every day, every week, month, and year. Think back now and make a list of the five biggest decisions you have had to make in the last five years.

Over the last five years my big decisions have included:

1. _____

2. _____

3. _____

4. _____

5. _____

What makes these decisions *big?* The expense they involved? The amount of time they consumed? The changes they required you to make in your lifestyle or career? The risks involved?

Next to each of those decisions, write down the factors involved that made each of them so significant:

| The Decision | What Was Involved |
|---|---|
| 1. _____ | _____ |
| 2. _____ | _____ |
| 3. _____ | _____ |
| 4. _____ | _____ |
| 5. _____ | _____ |

In looking back at these decisions and all that was involved, how do you feel now about the decisions you made? Did you make a good decision, or a bad one? Note below whether each decision proved to be good or bad, and why.

| The Decision | It Was Good/Bad Because |
| --- | --- |
| 1. _____ | _____ |
| 2. _____ | _____ |
| 3. _____ | _____ |
| 4. _____ | _____ |
| 5. _____ | _____ |

Now, think about *how* you made those big decisions, the process you used. Was it the same process you normally use in making your smaller daily decisions, or was it a more complex, thoughtful process?

I am certain that you devoted more thought to whether or not to buy a new car than you gave to whether to put grape or strawberry jelly on your breakfast toast. Routine daily decisions are generally made on automatic pilot, for a significant reason: the alternative choices generally will produce very similar results that are compatible with your goals. Whether you go with the grape jelly or strawberry, you will still have tasty toast. Red dress or blue dress, you'll be property attired.

But the choice of whether to spend a large amount of money for a new car or simply to live with your old car offers two very different options. One is surely more compatible with your long-term goals than the other. If your long-term goal is to save enough money to invest in the stock market, you may decide that you can live with the old car. But if having a nice car is more compatible with your long-term goals—say you want to job-hunt in a city that is a long drive from your current home—you will probably purchase the car.

Making wise decisions is an integral part of life, and a major step in the Success Process. It's been said that we have no choice about our birth and none about death, but everything in between is ours to decide. The heart of the decision-making process lies in wisely choosing among the available alternatives: the fixer-upper house or the modern new apartment? the established business or the risky new venture? the long-term relationship or the exciting new acquaintance? Alternatives such as these require careful consideration. You have to devote more time to these decisions than to the run-of-the-mill decisions you face each day.

To make difficult decisions wisely, it helps to have a systematic *process* for assessing each alternative and its consequences— the potential impact on each aspect of your life. Having a process will help you make decisions that are consistent with your values and principles as well as your vision for a better life. Note that it is also vital that you understand the importance of carefully identifying *as many alternatives as possible* when making a decision, and that you be prepared to handle any *criticism,* which often accompanies a decision to make a change.

From the list you made above, choose one of the most difficult decisions you have had to make over the last five years and beside it list all of the alternatives you considered before making the decision:

The decision I faced was:_____

The alternatives I considered included:_____

_____

Now that some time has passed, were there any alternatives you did not consider that, in retrospect, you should have included in the process of making the decision? If so, what were they? _____

_____

Also, note what criticisms you were subjected to because of the decision you did make. Next to each, write down the source of the criticism:

**The Criticism**                    **The Critic**

_____        _____

_____        _____

_____        _____

_____        _____

One great advantage in making careful decisions is that you are generally subjected to less criticism when those around you see that you have put a lot of thought into it before finally acting. When you've been thoughtful, you are also well-prepared to respond to the criticisms. Keep in mind that when you announce a decision to someone, generally they are hearing it for the first time. This is new information for them, even though you may have been considering it for a long time. Therefore, their response is likely to be critical because they have not invested the same thought into it as you. They have not weighed the alternatives as you have. And so, you should not let their negative thinking affect you, not if you have made this decision carefully. Just as some primitive tribes used curses to plant negative thoughts in the minds of their enemies and to rob them of their confidence, the power of negative reactions and responses can cripple your ability to follow through on decisions that you have made carefully.

The amount of time and effort you invest in making a particular decision depends to a great extent on the importance *you* attach to it. Even with important decisions, however, many people too often follow the same casual process they use in daily decision-making. They don't open their minds to all of the alternatives that may be available to them, and they don't think through all of the possible ramifications of each alternative.

My friend Marcus made a decision recently to push for a better job at the bank where he works. He wanted the job because it paid better and opened up greater opportunities. Those are good reasons, but Marcus did not consider another possible ramification of the move. The new job was largely one that paid on commission rather than straight salary. When business slowed down, Marcus discovered that his salary actually dropped from his previous position. Worse yet, when the market slowed even more, Marcus was laid off! He would not have been as vulnerable to a layoff in his old position. In making his decision, Marcus had failed to consider those possibilities, and it cost him dearly. Had Marcus followed a thoughtful decision-making process, he probably would have foreseen the negative possibilities. Now, he may have decided to take the new job anyway, but at least he would have been prepared for the negative turn of events.

## USING YOUR MIND AND YOUR HEART

There is another reason to carefully consider the big decisions in your life. Important matters require that you consider them both with your *mind* and with your *heart*. Your emotions cannot be put aside, and they should not be put aside when it comes to making big decisions in your life.

Even after you have intellectually weighed a decision and carefully thought it through, there remains the matter of what you feel in your heart. Some call this your "gut instinct," which sounds a little crude, but it is an instinct based on past experiences and the emotional value you place on a decision.

In *Emotional Intelligence*, Daniel Goleman notes that these gut instincts, or "somatic markers," are emotional signals that most often alert us to the potential hazards of certain courses of action, but "they can also alert us to a golden opportunity." Most of the time, we don't immediately recall what past experience or recollection triggers the gut instinct reaction, but generally we follow that instinct based on the emotions it sets off. Goleman believes the key to sound personal decision-making is to be attuned to your feelings. When you have a step-by-step process such as the one I am going to provide you for thoughtfully making the big decisions in your life, it helps ensure that you intellectually *and* emotionally weigh *all* of the relevant information and the best available alternatives to move you ahead in the Success Process.

There is one more aspect of decision-making that you need to consider before I introduce you to my process. I am going to ask you to *smile* while you go through it. I know that may sound silly, but science is on my side on this one too, according to those who have seriously studied what was once considered the province of motivational and inspirational writers and speakers. Nearly fifty years after Dr. Norman Vincent Peale wrote *The Power of Positive Thinking*, behavioral scientists and others have come around to *his* way of thinking. Science once scoffed at the notion that a positive or optimistic emotional approach to life could seriously affect your physical and mental health, but not anymore. Research has shown time and time again that optimism not only is an extremely helpful tool; it also is one that can be learned. Negative thinking can cripple you mentally, spiritually, and physically, and it can also impede your ability to make decisions wisely. An optimistic and positive emotional approach to decision-making, on the other hand, contributes to a more thoughtful and balanced consideration of all the factors involved.

A positive approach to the decision-making process opens

your mind, makes you more flexible in your thinking and more capable of handling complex personal or business decisions. On the other hand, being in a foul mood can foul your ability to make a good decision. Negative moods tend to promote fearful, biased, and overly cautious decision-making. So, before you make any important decision in your life, make sure that you are in the proper mood. Behavioral scientists and others suggest that if your mood is down you should go to a funny movie, read a funny book, or socialize with upbeat people who make you laugh. Studies have shown that laughter prompts you to think more broadly and freely, which helps a great deal in making complex decisions with far-reaching impact.

Check your mood right now and make sure you are in a positive, upbeat frame of mind before reading the rest of this chapter. If you are not in the proper frame of mind, take a break to lighten up. You have my permission to go to a funny movie, read a humorous book or even the funny papers, or visit with a friend who makes you laugh. Only after you are feeling in good humor can you move on to the next section of this chapter. If I see one frown, I'm shutting this book!

## THE WINNING-BY-A-DECISION PROCESS

### Step One: The Weigh-In

The need to make a big and important decision generally becomes apparent after you have been exposed to information or an opportunity that somehow sheds new light or gives you a new perspective on your existing situation. This new information or perspective forces you to examine your situation and to *weigh* it in comparison to the possibilities of making a change.

You may have been perfectly happy with your old car until your mechanic informed you that the new exhaust system for it would cost $500. In a similar manner, I was fairly content in my job with the federal prison system until Bob Brown introduced me to the possibilities of a career in marketing and public relations. Suddenly, my vision for a better life expanded. I began to see how I could incorporate my love of sports with a career that still gave me the opportunity to work with people.

Now, sometimes the new information presented may force you to see that sticking with the old way or existing situation is even more risky than seeking change. The heavy smoker whose medical exam reveals serious lung damage will probably see the light and decide to change his behavior based on the new information, or else.

The key question to be considered at this stage in the decision-making process is: *Are the risks serious if I don't change?* If the answer is *no*, then you have no need to change; you have the option of continuing on your current path. Let's say, for example, that you are considering applying for a new job. If your current job is secure and pays you well enough to provide a comfortable life, then there would appear to be no *serious* risks involved in staying with the status quo. If, however, your current job is one that could be downsized, then there is definitely risk involved in not seeking another, more secure position.

If the answer to the weigh-in question is *yes*, that there is serious risk involved, then it is time to move to the next step of the process.

Write down a decision that you are currently facing and give it a weigh-in:

_____

_____

What are the risks you face if you don't make the change that this decision will bring? Are they serious risks? Write them here:

## Step Two: Suiting Up

The next step in the decision-making process is to identify as many suitable alternative solutions or courses of actions as possible. This is another stop in the Success Process where it is useful to let your imagination run wild, dreaming up as many possible solutions as you can, weighing them all, and picking and choosing those that might appear to work.

Don't try to do this on your own. Enlist members of your support team to help you, and seek expert advice if you can. Go to people you trust in your field of employment, bosses and co-workers, even competitors. Go to the library and check magazines and books that deal with your market. Get on the Internet and use one of the search mechanisms such as Netscape or Web Browser to see what information is available out there. At this point don't limit the alternatives; think of as many as you can by asking, "Is this an acceptable method for dealing with the challenge?"

Sticking with our example of trying to decide whether to apply for a new job, let's say that you've discovered that your company is going to downsize and there is a substantial risk that your position will be cut. What alternatives do you have other than applying for another job?

Let's list a few:

- Hold on to your current job and hope that it won't be cut.
- Hold on to your current job and hope that if it is cut, you will be moved to a comparable or better position rather than being fired.

- Hold on to your current job, get fired, but take the termination package, which includes a year's salary and company-paid retraining or college courses. Take advantage of this program and apply after you have obtained the additional training or education.
- Start your own business while still employed and then rely on money from your termination package to get by until it becomes profitable.
- Send out résumés to companies that offer similar positions.
- Use this opportunity to make a career switch and apply for a position in an entirely new area that interests you more.
- Get out of the job market entirely and stay home to take care of family members.

### Step Three: Checking the Fit

Once you have identified a wide range of suitable alternatives, the next step is to mentally try each one on and check to see which best fits your vision for a better life. This is a time to more carefully examine each alternative, to get a feel for them and to evaluate the pros and cons of each. Make sure you examine them for both the short term and the long term. If you don't find any alternatives that match up to your vision for a better life, you may have to go back to Step Two and come up with more attractive alternatives.

The key questions at this stage are: *Which alternative is best?* and *Can the best alternative meet the essential requirements?*

The appeal of the alternatives depends to a great degree upon your personal needs and goals. For example, if you are under thirty-five, you probably would be more inclined to take the retraining or college courses offered by the termination package. For people in that age bracket, the risk factor is probably not as high as for those over thirty-five. If you are over that age, you may feel that it is too late to take time out for retraining, but given the increasing emphasis placed on *continuous education* in the workforce, success may well depend on your willingness to grow and learn throughout your career. At this stage of the decision-making process it is important to try on each alternative to decide which best suits you.

An effective way to check the fit of each alternative is to create a *Decision Balance Sheet*. In the space below, write down one alternative that appears to be strong.

**ALTERNATIVE No. 1**

_____

_____

Now, list the pros and cons of this alternative in each category listed:

*Your Personal Life*

**PROS**                         **CONS**

_____          _____

_____          _____

_____          _____

_____          _____

*Your Job or Career*

**PROS**                         **CONS**

_____          _____

_____          _____

_____    _____

_____    _____

*Your Place in the Community*

**PROS** _____    **CONS** _____

_____    _____

_____    _____

_____    _____

_____    _____

Now, review the pros and cons in each area of your life. When you find one on each side that appear to balance each other out, cross them out. If you find one pro that seems to outweigh two cons, cross all three out. If you find two cons equal to three pros, cross out all five. Do this with every possible alternative until you decide which are simply unacceptable and which are the most acceptable by determining whether their impact on your life would be positive or negative overall. This is a subjective way of measuring their appeal to you, and if nothing else it prods you to thoroughly think through each alternative.

Note that there are two types of errors that you may be likely to make in completing the balance sheet:

1. You may overlook cons because you are reluctant to admit the potential for negative results.
2. You may be overly optimistic in projecting pros.

Remember that this has to be a thoroughly honest process, otherwise it is invalid. By being candid and thoughtful at this stage, you can save yourself a great deal of regret down the road.

## Step Four: Stepping into the Ring

At this point, you are like an actor taking on a role. After identifying the alternative—or alternatives, if you are torn between a number of choices—imagine yourself taking a particular course and take time to consider all of the implications.

Anticipate what might happen if you take this route with your life: What will the effect be on your personal relationships, your career, your place in the community? Will it mean relocating to another part of the country? Is that good or bad in terms of your overall lifestyle? Will it move you away from friends and family? Will it move you along toward your vision for a better life?

Sometimes, of course, you may have to take a side road in your journey along the Success Process. You may have to go to work for a smaller company a thousand miles away for a couple of years in order to get the experience that will help you get a job with the major corporation just down the street from where you want to live the rest of your life. So when you walk into the ring mentally with each alternative, always keep your ultimate goal in mind.

As you try out the most appealing alternatives, you will develop a sense of which is the most functional for you, and without even realizing it, you will move closer to making a final decision. Now the key question becomes: *Should I make the decision?*

## Step Five: Go for the Knockout!

Once you have committed to making a decision that you have carefully evaluated, you should be prepared to take it all the way without retreating. It is important to know going into it that there will be times when your decision will be challenged, but if you have followed each step in the process and given careful thought to your choices along the way, you should be able to face these challenges and overcome them.

Know, however, that these challenges may come. Others may disapprove of your decision because of their own biases and self-interest. The risks that you envisioned will probably arise, and maybe also some that you had not anticipated. It could be that the scenario you envisioned will not follow your vision. The benefits may not be as great or come as quick. The downside may be worse than you anticipated. The career fulfillment may be every bit as rewarding as you anticipated but the impact on your personal life may be much worse than you'd projected.

It is important to prepare yourself for such internal conflict and to always keep in mind your ultimate dreams of a better life. Very little is accomplished without at least some sacrifice and temporary setbacks. You may have to go deep into your reserves of patience and resilience to manage the change. But always keep in mind that you made the decision carefully and thoughtfully and that ultimately it should move you closer to your dreams and goals.

Finally, here is an inspirational poem by Robert Frost that may help you when you face a major decision.

## The Road Not Taken

*Two roads diverged in a yellow wood,*
*And sorry I could not travel both*
*And be one traveler, long I stood*
*And looked down one as far as I could*
*To where it bent in the undergrowth;*

*Then took the other, as just as fair,*
*And having perhaps the better claim,*
*Because it was grassy and wanted wear;*
*Though as for that, the passing there*
*Had worn them really about the same,*

*And both that morning equally lay*
*In leaves no step had trodden black.*
*Oh, I kept the first for another day!*
*Yet knowing how way leads on to way,*
*I doubted if I should ever come back.*

*I shall be telling this with a sigh*
*Somewhere ages and ages hence:*
*Two roads diverged in a wood, and I—*
*I took the one less traveled by,*
*And that has made all the difference.*

*Chapter 10*

# Commit to Your Vision

»»»»»»»»»»

*Not through height does one see the moon.*
African proverb

BEFORE I BECAME director of education at the federal prison in Chicago, which was a job that I enjoyed, I briefly had one of the worst jobs of my life. I transferred to Chicago from the federal prison near Denver, where I had been in an administrative job, but the only position available at the time in the Chicago facility was in Receiving and Discharge. I already had a master's degree in education, but I wasn't putting it to much use in this job. My duty was to help process and search inmates coming into and going from the prison. Obviously they weren't real happy to be there, and neither was I.

I hated that job with a passion, but I never let anyone know it. It may well have been one of the worst jobs in the building, but I had the best attitude of any employee there. My co-workers and supervisors would ask how it was going and I would tell them, "Great, just great." I was determined not to complain. Instead, I committed myself to being such a positive and dedicated employee that my supervisors would have no choice but to promote me. You see, it was no secret that my job was one of the most unpleasant in the prison. Everyone knew it. So I would not have made much of an impression by reinforcing what everyone already knew. I decided to make an impression instead by committing myself to that job.

My plan was to show that I could stand out even in a bad position. Since the rewards of the job were nonexistent, I looked around for other opportunities to show my leadership abilities. I became president of the employees' club and worked in my off hours to make conditions better for my co-workers. I contributed to the employee newsletter. I did everything I could to rise above my circumstances and to focus instead on the possibilities.

It worked. One day the warden came by and asked how I was doing in my job and I told him I was doing the best I could to make everything run smoothly for him. Within a very short time, I was asked to apply for the job of supervisor of education at the prison. My boss told me that I had impressed everyone with my positive attitude toward a job that they knew I must have found unchallenging. I changed my circumstances by committing myself to rising above a bad situation. My goal was to do that bad job so well that my supervisors would have to promote me, and they did.

There is great power in making a commitment to bettering your life. When you dedicate yourself to rising above your circumstances, you will rise. When you let the people around you know that you not only *want* something better, you are *dedicated* to it, they buy into your vision of yourself. They become your cheerleaders and champions.

Why is it that we cheer the underdogs in sporting events and movies? Why do the benchwarmers who play with enthusiasm draw cheers as great as the stars when they enter a game? Because the fans sense a *commitment* to the game in those players too. They want to reward that commitment. That is part of the human spirit. We want to see those who strive succeed.

## COMMITTING TO BETTERING YOUR LIFE

We are now at the final step of the Success Process. I have offered you suggestions on how to:

- Increase your self-awareness so that you are in control of emotions and feelings that may have held you back in the past.
- Create a vision of your dreams and goals.
- Develop a plan to pursue those goals.
- Come up with your own Rules of the Road to stay focused on your plan without losing sight of the people and principles that are important to you.
- Take the risks necessary to move forward.
- Manage your responses to changes brought on by taking risks.
- Build a support team to assist you in dealing with changes in your life.
- Make wise decisions.

The final step in the Success Process is to make a *total commitment* to your vision for a better life and the all-out pursuit of it. That means never giving up, never giving in, never losing your focus and your desire to better yourself, whether in regard to your relationships, your job or career, or your role as a positive force in your community.

Each of the steps I have provided you is vital, and the final one is perhaps as important as any of them because if you don't fully commit yourself to bettering your life, how will you ever rise above difficult circumstances and obstacles in your path?

What does it mean to make a commitment? I have been reminded of the power of commitment in recent weeks as I watched the 1996 summer Olympic Games in Atlanta. The Olympics provide a wealth of examples of the power of committing to a dream. From tiny gymnasts who put their personal pain aside to compete for the glory of their teammates, to the people of Atlanta who succeeded in pulling off an incredible feat in bringing the international games to their community, the most recent Olympics provided countless tales of, as the theme song went, *the power of the dream.*

Although most people focus on who will win medals at the Olympics, some of my favorite Olympic memories are from a year in which the United States had one of its worst medal performances in modern history. The United States brought home only two gold medals and just six medals altogether from the winter Olympics in Calgary, Canada, in 1988. For me, though, it was perhaps one of the greatest displays of the true Olympic spirit, courage, and the power of commitment.

Two Olympians from Calgary stood out, not so much for how they performed, but for how committed they were to their dreams of athletic achievement. One of them was Dan Jansen, the young man from West Allis, Wisconsin, who had been the favorite to win the gold in both the 500 and 1,000 meter speed skating events. Just seven hours before his first race started, however, Dan's sister Jane died of leukemia. Her death had not been unexpected, but it was still devastating for Dan, who had been extremely close to her. He decided to skate and to dedicate his performance to her memory, but when he stepped up to the starting line for the 500 meter race, he appeared to be dazed.

The emotional anguish in his expression and the obvious inner battle between his feelings for his sister and his desire to compete made for a powerful moment. People around the world were moved by the courage he showed in even attempting to race. Perhaps not everyone wanted Dan Jansen to win that race, but I think I can safely say that no one was rooting for him to lose.

He did lose, however. Distracted by the tragedy of his sister's death, he tripped and fell shortly into the race. His powerful body simply could not carry the weight of his shattered emotions. Then, three nights later, the world was pulling for him again as he got off to a winning pace in the 1,000 meter event. But again the inner turmoil took its toll. With the world watching, this great athlete fell again. Dan Jansen failed, but he was not defeated. He was still committed to his dream. "I'll be back," he promised his supporters.

Olympic officials rewarded Jansen's courage and his obvious commitment to his sport by giving him the Olympic Spirit Award that year. After having difficulty and performing poorly in the 1992 Olympics, Jansen honored his commitment by staying in competition for the 1994 Olympics. There, although he very nearly fell again, Dan set a world record and took the gold in the 1,000 meter. Jansen's commitment to his sport and to his own athletic ability is inspiring and moving. The world's reaction to his struggle and his ultimate achievement of his vision for Olympic gold says a great deal to me about our high regard for commitment, and so does the response to another courageous athlete at Calgary, whose performance prompted as much laughter as Jansen's provoked tears.

Unlike the powerfully built Jansen, this athlete was a strange bird who wanted to fly, and believe me, even though he could barely get off the ground, his spirit soared. Blind in one eye, with the athletic grace of an albatross in a headwind, Eddie "the Eagle" Edwards, a plasterer by trade, was the first British ski jumper in Olympic history, which was not surprising, since England has no ski jumps. Eddie was twenty-four years old and had only been ski jumping two years when he committed to his vision of competing in the Olympic games.

He had no coach, no financial support, no equipment. So, he chopped wood, washed dishes, swept floors, and ate table scraps to save money so that he could train in Finland for the 1988 Olympics. Still, he had so little money that he lived in a mental hospital there because the rate was only $2 a night.

In truth, Eddie the Eagle was not an Olympic caliber ski

jumper. But he had heart and commitment to a dream, and every time he stood at the top of the jump, people all over the world cheered that he would surpass his own dreams and win an Olympic medal. Eddie did have his best jump ever in the 90 meter competition. It was a mere 155 feet, 10 inches short of the winning jump, but the crowd cheered as though Eddie the Eagle had set a world record.

Why did so many people cheer this poor, nearsighted plasterer? Eddie knew. "People had read about the struggle I had to make the Olympics, which was my dream, and they could see that dreams come true," he said afterward. When we cheer for underdogs such as Eddie the Eagle, we are applauding their drive, their positive energy, their vision, and, most of all, their commitment to their dreams and goals. I told you earlier of my assistant Chris, who wanted to gain experience in sports marketing so badly that he offered to work for free. In communicating his commitment to me, Chris created positive energy that charged me up and made me accept his vision of himself. I plugged into Chris's dream because of that positive energy. Out of nothing—no experience, no job opening—he changed his circumstances. He bettered his life with nothing more than his commitment.

How could Chris take such a risk? How could Dan Jansen ever have found the strength to continue his athletic career through three Olympics, unless he was totally committed to his dream of winning a gold medal? How could Eddie the Eagle have found the courage to fly, if it were not for his great commitment to simply competing in the Olympics?

A commitment is not some vague promise to yourself that you will do something. A commitment is something you *live*. Everything you do is a reflection of your commitment. Every approach you take to your life, the good times and the hard times, is an expression of that commitment. A true commitment is the focusing of energy toward a purpose or cause. It is *doing* rather than *say-*

*ing*. It is persevering and continuing to pursue your vision in spite of distractions, hardships, criticism, and risk. It is doing something because you believe it is right for you to do it. Why is this so important? Because the commitments you choose to make and to fulfill in your life ultimately determine how the value of your life is judged.

You can make a lot of mistakes on the journey to a better life without seriously jeopardizing your ability to achieve your dream. But it will not happen if you make the mistake of failing to commit yourself fully to your vision. No one can help you overcome a lack of commitment to your own life. If you don't have it, no one can provide it for you. You must demand it of yourself.

Write down some commitments you have made already in your life, such as your commitment to your family, to your friends, to a relationship, to a social cause, or to a career path.

I have committed to: _____

_____

_____

_____

_____

Next, for each commitment that you have *kept*, note what the positive results have been in your life.

| COMMITMENT | RESULT |
| --- | --- |
| | |
| | |
| | |
| | |

The commitments in your life obviously have a great impact on the quality of life you lead. Being committed to goals and principles and to living a better life creates positive energy that affects all areas of your life. Other than my commitment to myself, I had absolutely no reason to dig in and give my best effort to that terrible job in Receiving and Discharge. No reason other than a commitment to creating positive energy that would propel me right out of that job. What if I had decided that the job was not worth my effort? What if I had gone to my supervisors and said, "This job is beneath me"? Would that have made me a more valuable employee in their eyes?

I made a commitment when I took that job to do it to the best of my abilities. If I had failed to honor that commitment, I would have dishonored myself. I believe that anytime you fail or abandon a commitment, you lose a little of yourself.

You can't fake commitment. Either you put everything into it or you don't. Have you ever witnessed someone competing in a game that they weren't really committed to winning? It wasn't hard to pick that person out, was it? That person may have *thought* he was committed to playing, but his actions demonstrated the reality. To really understand the difference between being *committed* and simply being *involved*, I suggest you take a look at your next breakfast. Check out your ham and eggs on the plate. Now think about the source of the ham and the source of the eggs. Then, consider this: that pig was fully committed, while the chicken was merely involved.

Commitment is giving all that you have to get all that you want. So many people who are unhappy with their lives or circumstances miss this point. They seem to think the answer is to complain, but what good does it do to attack a negative situation with negative attitudes and behavior? That approach reflects a *victim's mentality*. Victims blame. They foster resentment and anger. And they just don't get it.

Nobody cheers for a player with a bad attitude. The bosses don't look to promote the worker who complains or does a tough job poorly. The world in general does not respond to negative energy. Each of the steps I have offered in the preceding chapters is essential, but, like the individual ingredients in a cake recipe, no one of them will produce the desired results by itself. You need to live each of them and you need one more thing. Just as those ingredients in a recipe have to be put to the flame to create the cake, you must provide the spark of commitment to produce the energy that will transform your life.

As anyone who has ever made a New Year's resolution knows, it is easy to make commitments, but hard to keep them. Write down any commitments you have made that you have not honored:

_____

_____

_____

What sort of positive energy came out of those unfulfilled commitments? Do I need to even provide a line for your response? I don't think so. Making a commitment is like exercising a muscle; it has to be worked and tested and strengthened over time. If you make small commitments such as keeping the house clean, mowing the yard, and eating right, and then don't keep them, how will you honor your greater commitments, to yourself and others? Commitment is a capacity for setting goals and achieving them. That capacity can be enlarged only through exercising your power to make commitments and fulfilling them.

Write down some small commitments that you can make in the next few days and weeks in order to build your power to keep commitments. For example, commit to reading an inspiring book about someone such as Nelson Mandela, who committed his life to freeing his nation from apartheid, or Martin Luther King, who fought for civil rights and changed this nation just as Mandela changed his.

In the next week, I commit to three actions that will move me closer to my vision of a better life:

1. _____

2. _____

3. _____


## HONORING YOUR COMMITMENTS

Keeping a commitment is a major step forward, but breaking one is a step back. It is vital that you don't make commitments that you can't keep; otherwise you will never advance toward your vision of a better life. So you should make them wisely and only after careful consideration. If you overload yourself with responsibilities, you will succeed only in frustrating yourself and those around you.

Commitments that are kept build your confidence and produce changes that help you break free of the circumstances that have held you back. Stephen Covey teaches that the first step in getting unstuck with your life is to *stop breaking commitments to yourself.* If you tell yourself you are going to do something, you have to do it; otherwise you'll never be free to pursue your vision of a better life.

You have to have confidence in your ability to translate commitments to positive action. Also, you will never become capable of honoring your commitments to others if you can't keep them to yourself. Failing yourself is one thing, failing others is another.

Imagine volunteering to coach a Little League team and then failing to show up. How many lives are affected when that sort of commitment is not fulfilled?

When you keep your commitments, you build trust in yourself, and with others. Commitments are promises, and each commitment that you make and stick with is a goal achieved. Each goal that you achieve is another indication that you are guided by the possibilities of your life, rather than the circumstances.

Too many people give only lip service to "making a commitment." They mentally embrace the concept without involving themselves emotionally in the action. Making a commitment means devoting your time, money, and effort to achieving compelling objectives. Commitments can be very broad and involve virtually all aspects of your life—a commitment to raise your children, for example. They can also be very specific—a commitment to rent an apartment for a year. But all commitments are directed toward achieving specific *results*. A committed person is goal-oriented. A committed person has *vision* and is *enthusiastic* about avidly pursuing that vision. Emerson said, "*Nothing great is ever achieved without enthusiasm.*"

*Enthusiasm* comes with an emotional commitment to a vision, goal, or dream. It comes when you pursue your goals as if your life depends on it, and it does. Understand, your life depends not on your goals, but on your *pursuit* of those goals, because when you are leading a life with direction and purpose and enthusiasm, you are truly *living*. Think about the people you know who seem to be just going through the motions of life. What do they have in common? They lack direction. They have no enthusiasm. The thought of a challenge sends them fleeing in terror back to their La-Z-Boy recliners, back to the bar stool, back to the street-corner hangout, back to a life going nowhere fast.

Now, think about the people you know who are full of life. What do they all share? A purpose and direction. An enthusiasm for life. A joy in what they are doing. A willingness to face challenges and overcome them. An enthusiasm bred of an emotional commitment to a vision for a better life. Being mentally and emotionally committed to *enthusiastically* pursuing your vision for a better life is vital for five reasons.

## 1. MEETING CHALLENGES

There are two ways to respond when your vision for a better life is challenged. You either give up or step up. The person who is enthusiastic and committed to bettering his or her life steps up and accepts challenges as opportunities for growth. The uncommitted individual retreats. Enthusiasm for your goals and dreams generates the energy you need to overcome obstacles in your path along the Success Process. In the overwhelming majority of cases, this process is a long-distance run, not a short sprint. You can't expect to achieve your dreams with a short burst of speed. Only a deep emotional commitment and the enthusiasm and energy that come with it will get you through the long haul.

## 2. DEVELOPING YOUR TALENTS

When you bring emotional commitment and enthusiasm to your pursuit of a better life, you create an environment in which all of your talents are nurtured, developed, and put to their highest use. Why do so many people go to their graves with their talents and gifts untapped? Think about that next time you walk past a cemetery. How might the world be different had everyone gone to their graves only after their talent had been allowed to fully blossom? That is accomplished only by commitment and enthusiasm, by constantly striving to better your life by tapping into the deepest reserves, pulling out all that is within you and unleashing those gifts granted you.

## 3. REVVING UP FOR RISKS

Imagine yourself on a bridge over a river, say the Michigan Avenue bridge over the Chicago River in the heart of the great city of Chicago. As you cross the bridge, you look down and see a piece of paper floating by. It's just a scrap of notebook paper, so you pay it no heed and continue on your way. It doesn't enter your mind to dive into the water and retrieve that piece of paper.

Now, look again. Instead of a simple scrap of paper, you realize that piece of paper is a check written out to you for $1 million. Suddenly, you are *emotionally* engaged. That amount of money could change your life. It would wipe out all of your unpaid bills and give you the security to pursue your greatest dreams in your life. For that, you not only are willing to consider taking a risk, you are *enthusiastic* about taking that risk. You find yourself leaping over the railing and swimming after the check because you have a vision of what that piece of paper can do for your life, and so you have become emotionally and enthusiastically *committed* to the goal of retrieving that money before it floats out of sight.

Emotional commitment and enthusiasm have that effect on people. It revs them up to take the risks that are essential to the pursuit of their goals and dreams. Without them, you can't see the value of taking risks and therefore you are not willing to make the leap. If you don't have your heart in your pursuit of a better life, you won't be willing to take the risks that are essential.

## 4. DEVELOPING EXCELLENCE

A friend told me recently about finding commitment to excellence in a most unusual place—a state driver's license examining station in a strip shopping mall in Peoria. It seems that this particular examining station employed a fellow named Earl Dempsey, who had retired from a job as a coffee company salesman and started a new career as the photographer for driver's license photographs. After seventeen years in that job, and at the age of seventy-eight, Dempsey was still exhibiting such emotional commitment and enthusiasm in his work that people from all over Illinois drove to *his* station to have their driver's license photographs taken, according to a newspaper story about him.

"In this fast-paced world you don't find many people like him," said Dempsey's boss.

The story noted that the experience of taking driver's license exams and having your photograph taken is almost universally regarded as one of the most unpleasant and aggravating requirements of government—except at Dempsey's station. Although he was only one of many employees, there was no doubt that Dempsey and his spirit were the dominant forces of this place. His good humor, gentlemanly manner, nonstop patter, and really bad jokes affected everyone there. Even his co-workers, who had undoubtedly heard the same jokes hundreds of times, loved Dempsey because of his enthusiasm and commitment to his work. People actually *smiled* in their driver's license photos taken by him, because by the time they'd filled out all the forms and taken the tests they'd become infected with his enthusiasm.

Dempsey brought excellence to such a mundane place because he committed himself to it with enthusiasm. He made a generally unpleasant experience so much more fun that some families made it a tradition to have him take their driver's license photographs. The fact that newspapers and television news shows were drawn to do stories on Dempsey illustrates how people are attracted and inspired by those who are committed to excellence. It also illustrates, sadly, how few people have that sort of commitment in their lives.

If Dempsey's driver's license examining station could become the sort of place that people actually looked forward to visiting, why couldn't all of them be that way? The answer, of course, is that most employees in such places are just there to get the job done, get through the day, and a collect paycheck at the end of the week. This is true in so many businesses today. There is very little *service* in the service economy, very little quality in the products we purchase. That is why so many extended warranties are sold these days. People no longer expect the products they purchase to function the way they should.

Dempsey stood out with his commitment, and so will you. A few years ago, there were hundreds of newspaper articles about a growing department store chain that emphasized a commitment to customer service above all else. As a result, towns practically begged Nordstrom to locate stores within their boundaries. Enthusiasm and commitment generate excellence, and that leads to success. Other department store chains may have given lip service to customer satisfaction, but Nordstrom went all out, and it profited greatly from that commitment.

## 5. NOBODY MAKES IT ALONE

Enthusiasm and passion brought to a commitment inspire excellence, and excellence in turn inspires others to care about your commitment. Think back to the teacher or coach or mentor who played an important role in your life. What distinguished this person from all the others that you came into contact with growing up? Caring and commitment. The teachers who care about their students and bring enthusiasm and excellence into the classroom inspire the same caring and excellence in their students. Coaches who demand excellence inspire it in their players, as do supervisors and CEOs. When you bring passion to your commitment, you inspire others to share your vision and to look for ways to help you along. Enthusiasm is the match that lights the fire of commitment in you and in those around you.

A commitment to pursue a better life is vital to your journey along the Success Process, but there are four other commitments that are also essential:

## 1. *Commit to celebrating your successes.*

At first glance, you may think this sounds a little silly—who wouldn't commit to a successful life? The truth is, however, that often people are not prepared for success when it comes. Sometimes they feel undeserving of success, unworthy of it, and they can't handle it. They self-destruct. Be aware of this, and understand that it is necessary to celebrate your successes. I know, that may seem like the least of your problems early in the Success Process, but as I have said throughout this book, to get where you want to go in life, you must become who you need to be. If you don't feel as though you deserve to sit in the vice president's or CEO's chair, you won't be in it long. If you don't feel worthy of the love of someone who loves you, you may sabotage the relationship.

Commit to success by earning it and knowing that you deserve it. Prepare yourself so that when success comes, you are comfortable with it. Learn to celebrate your successes and acknowledge your defeats, but then move on to the next opportunity and challenge.

## 2. *Commit to continuous spiritual, intellectual, and emotional learning.*

One commitment I have is my belief in lifelong learning. This refers not so much to formal education as self-education: reading, traveling, exploring new fields, new training, and continuous personal, spiritual, and intellectual learning. This is not a luxury like a Florida condo. The U.S. Department of Education reports that today most adults will have at least three significant job changes in their lifetime. That means you will need to keep your mind sharp by continuously developing your ability to absorb new information while striving to build your emotional and spiritual strength to handle all that life throws at you.

How do you do this? By seeking knowledge. A study on reading habits by the publishing industry recently found that the laziest readers are young adults under the age of twenty-five. People in this category purchase only 4 percent of all books sold. Now, the study noted that it may be that this age group buys fewer books because it has less disposable income than others. I hope so. As someone who did not become an avid reader until relatively late in life, I realize the importance and value of lifelong learning through reading.

Once I began reading as much as I could find about my areas of interest, it opened my world up for me. I realize now that one reason I was not where I wanted to be in life was that I hadn't made the effort to find out how to get there by reading and learning.

At the beginning of this century, the majority of the people in this country were involved in agriculture. By the middle of the century, the majority were involved in some sort of industrial or factory work. And now, as this century closes and a new one is about to dawn, we have shifted to what some are calling the *Knowledge Age.*

"Knowledge has become the key resource for economic strength. Knowledge knows no boundaries. There is no domestic knowledge and no international knowledge. There is only knowledge. It is not tied to any country. It is portable. It can be created everywhere, fast and cheaply. And it is, by definition, changing," wrote Peter C. Drucker in a widely noted *Atlantic Monthly* article.

Knowledge has become the key resource in our global economy, and this means it is vital that you commit yourself to *continual education.* What you know and how quickly you act on it will be the primary factor in your level of achievement. You have to know what is going on in the world around you because in this global society so many things are interrelated. That is why newspapers and Internet services are developing specialized newspapers that can be customized to your needs and accessed instantly any time of the day.

When you commit to lifelong learning and act on that commitment by constantly keeping abreast of the issues and areas and interests that are important to your growth and development, you are also committing to bettering your life. The great Frederick Douglass recognized this fact even in his time, when he said, "When you are working with your hands, they grow larger. The same is true for your heads. Seek to acquire knowledge as well as property."

## 3. *Commit to helping others pursue a better life.*

Along with committing to your own success, I'd advise you to commit also to spreading success and enhancing the lives of others, particularly those who are still struggling to find their own way. Throughout this book, I have advised you to always consider not only your personal relationships and your job or career but also your role in the community as you pursue a better life. You don't have to wait until you are on top to do it. My mother, Mary Graham, founded a support group for families dealing with mental retardation and over the years has won many community service awards. Ten years ago, I followed her lead when I founded the nonprofit Athletes Against Drugs as part of my commitment to the community.

I did it because I'd grown angry at seeing so many reports in the media about athletes who were using drugs and destroying their lives. There were not a lot of role models who looked like me when I was growing up in Whitesboro. But in the sports pages and on television there were black athletes such as Wally Jones and Wilt Chamberlain and Julius Erving, who served as my role models. It sickened me to see athletes of similar stature being arrested or blowing careers because of drug use. Worse, however, was the growing notion that drug use was something to be admired and duplicated by young people. So many young men and women appear to be overwhelmed by poverty, low self-esteem, broken families, and a lack of structure in their lives. They turn to gangs, guns, violence, substance abuse, and other antisocial and self-destructive outlets for their feelings of anger and powerlessness. So many young people look to athletes and sports as the only positive outlet for their energies and attentions, I wanted to show them a way out by offering positive role models. I knew that the vast majority of successful athletes were not drug users and I wanted to create a forum for them to serve as role models and advocates for a healthy, positive lifestyle.

I was in my early thirties, without a lot of money, but I believed strongly in the concept of Athletes Against Drugs and when I committed myself to creating this forum for positive role models, I discovered that others were willing to embrace the idea. Believe it or not, the first guy I signed up was a young basketball player on the Chicago Bulls named Michael Jordan. We had met when I served as his stand-in for the making of a Chevrolet commercial in Chicago. As you might imagine, it wasn't easy for the producers to find a stand-in of the same height and build as Michael Jordan, but I had done a few commercials around town, so they asked me. Michael and I had been friends since the days when he first arrived in town as a little-known rookie out of North Carolina. In fact, he gave me my first set of season tickets to the Bulls games in the old Chicago Stadium.

Michael was not difficult to recruit for Athletes Against Drugs. I simply wrote down my concept on a piece of paper and asked him if he would be willing to support it. He signed right up. Athletes Against Drugs now has more than 150 members, ranging from Olympic athletes to top professional golf and tennis players, and professional football, basketball, and baseball stars. The athletes make a commitment to participate in programs for schools and youth organizations so that youngsters can have positive alternatives to drugs, crime, and gang membership. Athletes Against Drugs teaches young people that there is a better life out there, and it helps them take the first few steps along the Success Process by building their self-esteem and self-development by providing goal-oriented activities.

This book is an outgrowth of my involvement with young people in not only Athletes Against Drugs but also Junior Achievement. These organizations and several others I am involved with provide me the opportunity to fulfill my commitment to the community, and believe me, I get as much out of them as they get out of me.

The commitments you make to yourself and to others—whether they are individuals or organizations—are the path marks you make on your journey toward your vision of a better life. Every commitment that you fulfill is a goal achieved. When others in your community see that you honor your commitments, they come to perceive you as someone who makes a difference, someone with positive energy who brings success to all aspects of his or her life. That is why I encourage you to participate in charitable and community organizations. Do it for yourself and for others.

Bob Shannon, the former high school coach in East St. Louis, Illinois, offers another example of the value of committing your life to the success of others. In a *Chicago Tribune* article, writer Barry Temkin described Shannon as an unlikely but genuine hero. "He is aloof. He is dogmatic. He is occasionally given to seeing enemies where there are none. Yet few men are more heroic," wrote Temkin.

What was it about Bob Shannon's career at East St. Louis High School that made him so respected that sports reporters praised him and an entire book, *The Right Kind of Heroes*, was written about him? After all, he was nothing more than a head football coach at a high school in a town so poor that its city hall was once sold off because the town didn't have enough money to pay a judgment against it. East St. Louis High School is itself so poor that the showers don't work, the lockers lack doors, and the playing equipment is so shoddy it is sometimes difficult to tell who is dressed to play and who is just hanging on the sidelines. Without the money to paint markings on the football field, Shannon had to burn the yardage markers and sidelines into the grass with weed killer that he pays for himself.

Coach Shannon knew how to make do when you have to do without. He grew up in a Mississippi cabin with cracks in the floor so wide he could see the chickens nesting beneath the house. One of eleven children and with a widowed mother, he worked odd jobs to pay his own way through college, where playing football was his means to the end of getting an education. Shannon, who was once named national Coach of the Year, rose above that background, but that is not what made him so respected. Nor is it the fact that his coaching record over nineteen seasons in East St. Louis was 193-33 with six state titles and sixteen playoff appearances.

The heroic aspect of Coach Shannon's life lies not so much in what he did for himself; it lies more in what he did for the young people around him. He helped hundreds of young athletes pursue better lives by motivating them to get into college. He demanded of his players, most of whom came from impoverished families, that they make a *commitment* not only to their teammates and to winning, but also to bettering their lives.

"I am about commitment," he has said.

Coach Shannon was a winner "because the ultimate goal of his program is not so much winning football games as in making winners of his players. He wins because he demands the best of his players on and off the field. Because he preaches discipline, character, preparation and—most of all—being the right kind of person," Temkin wrote.

For this coach, it isn't how good you are as an athlete; what matters to him is what kind of person you want to become. On

Shannon's teams, players were cut from the team for lack of commitment. He once kicked a star quarterback off the team because the player refused to take off his earring. Leaders don't wear earrings in Shannon's book. They commit fully, or they don't play for this coach.

By sharing his commitment and demanding the same from his players, Coach Shannon enriches the lives of hundreds of young people and makes his community, and his world, a far better place.

Like Coach Shannon, Sheila Louison made a commitment to help others seek better lives. This Gardena, California, entrepreneur operates the nonprofit New World Computer Training Center, where unemployed, low-income adults can take two-month training courses in computer operating systems, word processing, spreadsheets, and desktop publishing. "They walk in the door knowing nothing about computers, and when they leave they will know everything they need to know for an entry-level position," Louison told *Emerge* magazine. The program, which also offers job hunting advice, résumé help, and other guidance, is funded by the city of Gardena at a cost of $2,000 per pupil. The business has twenty computers, half of which Louison paid for out of personal funds, even though she drew no salary from the business during its early days of operation in 1994. Above all else, she was committed to helping others.

## 4. Commit to growing up as a lifelong process.

There is a major misconception that probably 99 percent of the world's population of children and adults share, and that is the myth of growing up. People seem to think that when you reach a certain chronological age, you are a *grown-up*, a finished product, a completed work. Well, it is not so. We all need to grow continuously throughout our lifetimes. We all need to continually seek knowledge and to be always searching for ways to expand our consciousness spiritually, intellectually, and emotionally. We are never grown-up. We should always be *growing up*.

Know that when you commit to your vision, you must also commit to *continuous* growth. Stephen Covey refers to this never-ending striving to better your life and the world around you as the *upward spiral*. I have heard others describe it as *living peak to peak*. Both are descriptions of a continuous cycle of growth in which every goal you attain becomes a springboard to a higher level of achievement.

You grow by constantly renewing your commitment to bettering yourself in all three Circles of Success: in your relationships, in your job or career, and in your community. Why should you strive to grow even after you have achieved a goal? Because that is what makes for a dynamic and rewarding life. Why sit life out if you can challenge yourself to develop your talents and skills even more? Why not take it all the way to the wall, using up every ounce of energy, every bit of creativity, every resource that the universe provides?

Listen to what your inner voice says. What does it tell you after you've sat around the house all day watching television? *I feel like a lump.* What does it say after you've cleaned the garage, mowed the lawn, cleaned up the yard, repaired assorted household appliances, and taken a five-mile jog? *I feel energized. I feel like I am accomplishing something.*

What will your list of accomplishments be at the end of your life? Will it be a long list? Listen to that inner voice, and cultivate it. Use the steps in the Success Process as your guidelines for pursuing a better life that forever follows the upward spiral. Why follow that path? Why would I care about how you live your life? Why should you care?

Look around you at the temptations and the distractions of the modern world. Think about how easy it is to give in to those corrupting influences. Why not just kick back and go where life takes you? Why not give in to all the seductions of drugs, gambling, pornography, and crime? Why should you commit to bettering your life? The answer is simple. If you don't, who will? If you don't pursue your vision of a better life, who is going to pursue it *for you?* If you choose to settle for less than what is possible for your life, you have no one else to blame for what you get. If you fall into the downward spiral of malaise—drugs, gambling, pornography, or crime—will the world cheer you on?  Will you fly like Eddie the Eagle? Or will you suffer the consequences of your own lethargy and lack of commitment?

Do you want the easy life? Take my road. Follow the Success Process, and even the hardest days will be easier than the best days you'll have in the downward spiral. Why? Because when you follow the Success Process, *you* are in control of your life. You decide where you are going, when you are going, and how you are going to get there. You are in control. A better life is always within your power to achieve.

And when you get to where you want to go, all you have to do is *commit* to reaching the next level of accomplishment, and then, once again, you will be on your way, upwardly mobile, to a better life.

As I stated at the beginning of this book, my goal was to teach you a process for pursuing success and a better life for yourself and for those around you. And as I noted then, I cannot guarantee success or happiness for you, or for myself, for that matter. Each of us can only dream and strive, and in the dreaming and striving, we may well achieve a better life.

I sincerely hope that you have found your journey through this book to be inspiring and rewarding as well as instructive. I'll be cheering and praying for you. Good luck on your journey.